THE 14TH KING GEORGE'S OWN SIKHS THE 1ST BATTALION (K.G.O.) (FEROZEPORE SIKHS), THE 11TH SIKH REGIMENT

1846–1933

COLONEL F. E. G. TALBOT

Edited By John Wilson & Stephen Ede-Borrett

Gosling Press

Copyright © F. E. G. TALBOT
This edition Copyright Gosling Press 2023
All rights reserved.
ISBN 978-1-874351-28-3 (Hardback)
ISBN 978-1-874351-29-0 (Paperback)

Gosling Press

www.goslingpress.co.uk

Front cover Watercolour of a 14th Sikhs Sepoy at Gallipoli
By kind permission of the artist Suman Kaur
https://sumankaur.co.uk

Introduction

The *History of the 14th Sikhs* has long been out of print and is a key history for those interested in the Indian troops at Gallipoli. This history written by Colonel Talbot has much greater coverage of the Regiment's Great War service than the 1948 one by Lieutenant Colonel Bamford which concentrates on the Second World War.

14th Ferozepore Sikhs was raised in 1846, after the First Anglo-Sikh War, from former soldiers of the Sikh army. The Regiment originally recruited local Sikhs and Punjabi Muslims but in 1866, the Punjabi Muslims were phased out and the Regiment became a single class regiment of Sikhs. In the 1922 reorganization, 14th Ferozepore Sikhs was designated 1st Battalion, 11th Sikh Regiment.

The Regiment is best known for their part in the Third Battle of Krithia at Gully Ravine on 4 June, with 12 out of 15 British officers and 11 out of 14 Indian officers recorded as casualties. In addition, they lost 380 NCOs and other ranks dead and wounded out of a strength of 514. By 6 July the Battalion was reduced to 2 officers and 117 men.

Writing of the Third Battle of Krithia during the campaign, General Sir Ian Hamilton paid tribute to the heroism of all ranks of the Regiment:

> In the highest sense of the word extreme gallantry has been shown by this fine Battalion... In spite of the tremendous losses there was not a sign of wavering all day. Not an inch of ground was given up and not a single straggler came back... The ends of the enemy trenches leading into the ravine were found to be blocked with the bodies of Sikhs, and of the enemy, who died fighting at close quarters, and the glacis slope is thickly dotted with the bodies of these fine soldiers all lying on their faces as

they fell in their steady advance on the enemy. The history of the Sikhs affords many instances of their value as soldiers, but it may be safely asserted that nothing finer than the grim valour and steady discipline displayed by them on 4th June has ever been done by the soldiers of the Khalsa. Their devotion to duty and their splendid loyalty to their orders and to their leaders make a record their nation should look back upon with pride for many generations. (*Gallipoli Diary*, 1926)

THE 14TH KING GEORGE'S OWN SIKHS THE 1ST BATTALION (K.G.O.) (FEROZEPORE SIKHS), THE 11TH SIKH REGIMENT

1846–1933

BY
COLONEL F. E. G. TALBOT

Edited by John Wilson & Stephen Ede-Borrett

THE TITLES OF THE REGIMENT

1846   The Regiment of Ferozepore.
1861   The 15th Regiment of Bengal Native Infantry.
1861   The 14th Regiment of Bengal Native Infantry.
1864   The 14th (Ferozepore) Regiment of Bengal Native Infantry.
1885   The 14th Regiment of Bengal Infantry (The Ferozepore Sikhs).
1901   The 14th (Ferozepore) Sikh Infantry.
1903   The 14th Ferozepore Sikhs.
1906   The 14th Prince of Wales's Own Ferozepore Sikhs.
1910   The 14th King George's Own Ferozepore Sikhs.
1922   The 1st Battalion (King George's Own) (Ferozepore Sikhs), the 11th Sikh Regiment.

CONTENTS

1	1846–1859	
	Early Days and The Indian Mutiny	1
2	1859–1893	
	Operations on The North-West Frontier	22
3	1894–1895	
	Waziristan and Chitral	37
4	1896–1914	
	The Tochi and China	52
5	1914–1915	
	The Great War: Egypt And Gallipoli, up to 27 June, 1915	66
6	1915	
	Gallipoli, 28 June–14 December 1915	87
7	1916–1918	
	Egypt, Bushire And Mesopotamia	105
8	1918–1919	
	The Great War: Mesopotamia (final phase)	120
9	1919–1933	
	India	140
	APPENDIX I	
	Commandants, 1846–1933	160
	APPENDIX II	
	British Officers, 1914	162
	APPENDIX III	
	War Casualties, 1914–1919	163
	APPENDIX IV	
	Drafts Sent to 14th Sikhs	165
	APPENDIX V	
	Subadar Majors, 1864–1934	166

Illustrations

I	Lucknow, 1857–1858	Pg 14
II	The North-West Frontier, India	Pg 41
III	The Gallipoli Peninsula, 1915	Pg 71
IV	The Gully Ravine, 4 June, 1915	Pg 80
V	The Battle Of Sari Bair, 7 August, 1915	Pg 96
VI	Mesopotamia, 1917–1918	Pg 110
VII	The River Tigris, October, 1918	Pg 125
VIII	The Peshawar Area	Pg 149

THE
BATTLE-HONOURS

LUCKNOW, ALI MASJID, AFGHANISTAN 1878–79,
DEFENCE OF CHITRAL, CHINA 1900,
AFGHANISTAN 1919

THE GREAT WAR
HELLES, KRITHIA, SUVLA, SARI BAIR
GALLIPOLI 1915, SUEZ CANAL, EGYPT 1915–16,
SHARQAT, MESOPOTAMIA 1917–18

CHAPTER I
1846–1859

EARLY DAYS AND THE INDIAN MUTINY

At the close of the First Sikh War in 1846, two Sikh irregular battalions were raised for service in the Bengal Army of the Honourable East India Company. One was designated the Regiment of Ferozepore and the other the Regiment of Ludhiana. They are now known as the 1st and 2nd Battalions of the 11th Sikh Regiment.

Recruits for the Ferozepore Regiment were enrolled from the cis-Sutlej area of the Punjab known as the Malwa country. They were gradually collected at Ferozepore, where Captain G. Tebbs took charge and became the first commandant. The date of his appointment was 1 August 1846.

The Ferozepore Regiment was organised in ten companies. Its establishment was fixed at four British combatant officers, one British surgeon, one British sergeant major, one British quartermaster-sergeant, two Indian doctors, twenty Indian officers and 1,140 Indian other ranks. Although an 'irregular' battalion, the uniform and headdresses were similar to that of regular units of the Bengal Army. The men wore a red tunic with yellow facings.

At the start, the majority of the Indian officers and two-thirds of the Non-commissioned officers were Purbiahs (Rajputs from Oudh) transferred from regular regiments of the Bengal Army. They were men who had been promoted for gallantry on active service. Soon, however, the majority of them reverted to their original corps. The recruits enrolled were mainly Sikhs, but also included some Mahommedans. Many had served in the old Khalsa (Sikh) Army.

One of the British officers who joined the Regiment at its formation was Ensign J. Brasyer; he was then thirty-six years old. Enlisting as a private in the East India Company's service, be had served as quartermaster sergeant with the 26th Bengal Native Infantry in the First Afghan War and First Sikh War and had recently been promoted to commissioned rank for gallantry and good service in the latter campaign. He had an intimate knowledge of Indians and their customs, and could speak their language fluently. His linguistic capacity was most useful, as he alone of the British officers with the newly-raised Regiment of Ferozepore was able to converse with the Sikhs in their own language.

In September 1846, the Regiment moved by route march from Ferozepore to Ambala. It was, of course, only partially trained and had not yet been armed. At Ambala, on 24 December, Colours were presented by the Commander-in-Chief, Lord Gough, and on 1 January 1847, the Ferozepore Regiment was armed with the smooth-bore percussion musket of the period.

At the end of 1848 the Battalion marched in relief from Ambala to Agra, where it was quartered for two years, moving thence to Meerut in October 1850.

The first commandant, Captain Tebbs, died in January 1852. He was succeeded by Captain T. E. Colebrooke.

In September 1852 the Battalion was selected for active service in Burma and started from Meerut for Calcutta. On the way, however, a cholera epidemic broke out. This not only caused sixty-six deaths in the Indian ranks, but prevented participation in the Burmese expedition. The Regiment reached Barrackpore in November and remained quartered there until the beginning of 1855, when it moved to Mirzapore. Whilst on the line of march to that place, Lieutenant Brasyer took over command of the Battalion from Major Colebrooke, who left India on retirement. The Ferozepore Regiment was still at Mirzapore on the outbreak of the Indian Mutiny in 1857.

THE INDIAN MUTINY, 1857–1858

The great mutiny of the Bengal Army is usually described as having started on 10 May 1857, the date of the outbreak at Meerut. For some time previously, however, there had been signs of unrest and disaffection. Rumours of this unrest had reached Lieutenant Brasyer, but during the early months of 1857 everything at Mirzapore was peaceful enough. With the Ferozepore Regiment there were present three British combatant officers, Lieutenant Brasyer (Commandant), Lieutenant A. W. Montagu and Lieutenant C. C. Taylor (Adjutant); also the regimental doctor, Surgeon J. Browne, and the two British non-commissioned officers, Sergeant-Major J. Brown and Quartermaster Sergeant J. Love.

On 7 May, Brasyer received telegraphic orders to move at once by forced marches to Allahabad with his headquarters and four hundred men. Leaving the remainder of the Battalion –not more than two hundred and fifty men, as many were absent on leave– at Mirzapore under Montagu, Brasyer marched off and entered the fort at Allahbad at daybreak on the 11th.

It may be worth recalling a few salient features of the situation in May 1857. The Army in India was not so homogeneous as it is today. Each Presidency– Madras, Bombay and Bengal –had its own separate army. Each army comprised troops of two categories: 'Royal' troops (i.e. units of the British regular Army) and the H.E.I.C.'s troops (which included both British and Indian units).

The Bengal Presidency stretched right across Northern India from Calcutta to Peshawar. Calcutta was the headquarters of the British Government. Oudh had only lately been annexed, and the Punjab was quite a recent acquisition. The bulk of the white troops were stationed in the Punjab. There were two British battalions at Calcutta, one at Dinapore – four hundred miles from Calcutta up the Ganges – one at Lucknow and at Agra. It was not till Meeru and Ambala were reached that the strength of the Europeans began to be in evidence.

Railways in India were in their infancy; in the Bengal Presidency the only railway line extended from Calcutta to Raniganj on the Ganges, a distance of one hundred and twenty miles. With the exception of a few trunk roads, the principal lines of communication were the great rivers such as the Ganges and Jumna and their large tributaries, and most of the cantonments lay on their banks. The heavier military stores were almost always carried by water.

ALLAHABAD

Allahabad was a most important strategic point, lying at the junction of the Ganges and Jumna Rivers, about five hundred miles distant from Calcutta. The two great lines of communication from Calcutta to the north-west, the River Ganges and the trunk road, passed close on either side of the Allahabad fort. The fort, moreover, contained an ordnance depot, stocked with large supplies of arms and ammunition. In the cantonment, two or three miles away, were quartered the 6th Bengal Native Infantry, a detachment of Oudh irregular cavalry and one company of Indian artillery. In the fort, apart from Brasyer and his Sikhs, there were sixty British invalid artillery pensioners, recently sent there, and a few commissariat and ordnance sergeants; while a guard of one hundred men of the 6th Native Infantry was on duty at the main gate, and another one hundred men of the same Regiment were distributed in guards at other gates and inside.

When news of the mutiny at Meerut on 10 May reached Calcutta, there was grave anxiety for Allahabad. 'Alahabad is one of the most anxious cases,' wrote Lady Canning, wife of the Governor-General, 'it is very important and there are no Europeans. Some invalids from Chunar have been sent to it and there are some very good Sikhs.'

At Allahabad itself, although in some minds there was certainly doubt and apprehension, the situation does not appear to have caused much anxiety at first. The Commissioner was optimistic. Colonel Simpson, commander of the troops and also commandant of the 6th Native Infantry, had implicit trust in his battalion, which bore a great reputation. Towards the end of May a company of Her Majesty's 84th Foot, the head of a stream of reinforcements being pushed up country from Calcutta, arrived at Allahabad; but it was not considered necessary to detain the British infantry there, and they continued their voyage by river to Cawnpore. It was not until 5 June that real precautionary measures were taken at Allahabad.

On that day an order came from the brigadier at Cawnpore to man the Allahabad fort with every available European. At the same time news was received of the mutiny two days earlier at Benares–a mutiny in which, owing to mismanagement, a Sikh battalion was involved–and Benares is only eighty miles distant from Allahabad.

All British women, children and non-combatants were now ordered into the fort; they numbered about two hundred and fifty. From the non-combatants a volunteer company about one hundred strong was formed. Colonel Simpson sent a company of the 6th Native Infantry, with a section of guns and a few cavalry, to guard the bridge of boats and prevent the rebels from Benares crossing the river. The danger mainly feared was from the Benares rebels, and there was anxiety lest the news of the disaffection of the Sikhs at Benares should affect the loyalty of Brasyer's Sikhs.

ALLAHABAD, 6 June

After dark on 6 June, 1857, the inmates of the fort heard the sound of musketry outside. Brasyer, who was thoroughly on the alert, quickly paraded his men under arms in readiness for emergency. Others in the fort, however, imagined that the rebels from Benares were being repelled by the loyal troops of Allahabad. The truth was soon known. The 6th Native Infantry had broken out and killed a number of their British officers. The artillerymen and Oudh irregular cavalry had joined the mutineers. Colonel Simpson, of the 6th, was wounded but succeeded in escaping to the fort.

Brasyer asked Colonel Simpson for instructions. Dazed and shaken, the latter told Brasyer to do as he pleased. Brasyer at once decided to disarm the 6th Native Infantry in the fort. He asked the officer in charge of the guard on the main gate to disarm his men. The men refused to give up their arms. Brasyer then moved forward, with his Sikhs in support, and ordered the men of the guard to pile arms and stand clear. They hesitated. One sepoy pointed his musket at Brasyer, but his Sikh orderly quickly knocked it aside. 'My men,' writes Brasyer in his Memoirs, 'with muskets at the ready and bayonets fixed now assumed a determined attitude and the mutinous guard then saw that they must give way.' The other guards of the 6th Native Infantry were disarmed by Brasyer without difficulty and the men were turned out of the fort. Meanwhile, an orgy of murder, rapine and incendiarism had started in Allahabad city. It continued for days. The mutinous troops were joined by all the town rabble, and their savagery was terrible.

The fort became subjected to a desultory siege, conducted only half-heartedly. A reinforcement of fifty men of the 1st Madras Fusiliers[1] arrived by river on 7 June, followed next day by another detachment. Finally, on the 11th, Colonel James Neill himself arrived with a third party of his battalion and took over command at Allahabad.

Prior to Neill's arrival the situation in the fort, though not critical, was most unsatisfactory. The nominal commander was wounded, much shaken and unfit to exercise control. The morale of many of the garrison was extremely low. Brasyer did what he could, but there were a number of officers senior to him and he was unable to exert much influence outside his own regiment: Neill, shortly after his arrival, on his own responsibility promoted Brasyer to the rank of captain – a step which was duly confirmed later by higher authority.

---

[1] The famous Blue-Caps later became the Royal Dublin Fusiliers.

Neill at once infused a new spirit into the fort garrison. By this time the whole countryside had broken out into insurrection. From 12 June onwards, Neill carried out a series of vigorous sorties against the rebels. He was quickly successful and, by measures of retribution, soon reduced the district to a state of trembling submission. British administration was re-established in Allahabad city on 17 June.

In the operations directed by Neill the Ferozepore Regiment took a prominent part. Casualties were not heavy; but they included the adjutant, Lieutenant Clarence Taylor, who was severely wounded on 13 June. Before the end of the month Lieutenant Montague, with the remainder of the Regiment from Mirzapore joined Brasyer at Allahabad.

Meanwhile, transport was being collected for a movement to the relief of Cawnpore; about one hundred and thirty miles farther up the Ganges. By 30 June sufficient had been procured to enable an advanced column, under Major Renaud of the Fusiliers, to start from Allahabad. This column included the headquarters and three hundred men of the Ferozepore Regiment. On the same day Brigadier General Henry Havelock arrived at Allahabad and took over command from Neill.

HAVELOCK's ADVANCE ON CAWNPORE

On 7 July, Havelock followed up Renaud with another column from Allahabad which included one hundred and thirty of the Sikhs. By this time news of the fall of Cawnpore had reached Havelock, and he sent orders to Renaud to stand fast pending reinforcement. He was overtaken on 12 July by Havelock, whose object now was to eject the rebels from Cawnpore as a preliminary to an advance from that place to the relief of Lucknow.

The combined forces under Havelock totalled less than two thousand troops, with eleven guns. The infantry units represented were the 1st Madras Fusiliers (376 strong), 64th Foot (435 strong), 84th Foot (190 strong), 78th Highlanders (284 strong) and Ferozepore Regiment (448 strong). Brasyer was the only British combatant officer present with his Sikhs, as Montagu had been left in charge of the detachment remaining at Allahabad. The British infantry were armed partially with Enfield rifles, except the Fusiliers who were wholly thus armed. The Sikhs had only the smooth-bore musket. Brasyer had previously at Allahabad permitted his men to discard their uniform caps and heavy tunics, and to wear instead the pugaree and ordinary Sikh blouse. The British troops were attired in their normal uniforms and headdresses, quite unsuitable for the Indian hot weather, except the Madras Fusiliers who wore a white smock instead of a tunic.

After overtaking Renaud, Havelock marched on a few miles and was preparing to camp on an open plain a few miles short of Fatehpur when a rebel force was seen advancing to the attack. Havelock retaliated by himself taking the offensive. The ensuing action was of short duration: for the accurate British gunfire and the superiority of the Enfield rifles was too much for the enemy who made but a feeble resistance before retreating in disorder with the loss of twelve guns. Our casualties were only fifteen in all.

Havelock halted his troops for a rest on 13 July, but was on the move again next day. On 15 July a strong body of rebels was ousted without difficulty from the village of Aong. Six miles farther on there was a bridge over a stream known as the Pundu Naddi. It was important to seize this before it could be destroyed, and Havelock pushed on despite the great heat. The bridge was secured, and the weary troops encamped within twenty-two miles of Cawnpore. Casualties in action on15 July totalled only twenty-six, but our soldiers were much exhausted by their efforts under a burning sun.

That evening Havelock received information that a large number of British women and children were held captive at Cawnpore, and he determined to push on without delay to effect their rescue. His efforts, unfortunately, were to prove fruitless, for the captives were murdered that same night.

Unaware of the tragedy, the force marched forward again at dawn on 16 July. The heat was exceptional, and only rendered the more oppressive by heavy rain. Fifteen miles had been traversed when the enemy was encountered in great strength in position covering

Cawnpore. After a reconnaissance, Havelock attacked the position in flank. Fighting continued till dark by which time the rebels were dispersed in confusion. The British force bivouacked for the night about two miles from Cawnpore cantonment. Battle casualties for the day totalled one hundred and eight (of which the Ferozepore Regiment incurred twelve) exclusive of numerous cases of heatstroke.

HAVELOCK AT CAWNPORE

Next morning the column marched in to Cawnpore. Owing to casualties and sickness there were now not more than fifteen hundred men fit for duty, and some rest was essential before Havelock could move on to the relief of Lucknow.

On 20 July, Neill arrived with a small body of reinforcements from Allahabad. The following days were spent in ferrying troops, transport and supplies across the Ganges. The river was unbridged and was at the time a broad, rapid and swollen torrent. Only one small steamer and a few boats were available for ferrying purposes.

Leaving Neill with three hundred men to hold an entrenched camp on the Cawnpore bank of the Ganges, Havelock by the 28th concentrated his striking force at Mangalwar, about five miles away on the far side of the river on the road to Lucknow, which was another forty-five miles farther on. The force was only fifteen hundred strong, with six guns; it included the head quarters and two hundred and fifty men of the Ferozepore Regiment.

The advance began at daybreak on 29 July. During the day Havelock covered eleven miles and fought two successful actions at Unao and Bashiratganj, capturing nineteen guns from the rebels who opposed him. But by nightfall he found that he had not more than eight hundred and fifty effective rifles left. In addition to eighty-eight casualties in action, many men had been struck down by the heat and by cholera. Moreover, ammunition was failing, there was news of the enemy at Lucknow having been reinforced, large rebel forces were threatening Neill at Cawnpore, and there was no prospect of the early arrival of any British reinforcements.

Havelock saw that he could not yet carry out his task. On 31 July he withdrew his force to Mangalwar.

On 5 August, however, he again moved forward and once more drove the enemy out of Bashiratganj. The British casualties were slight, twenty-five in all, but with cholera still rampant, Havelock again realised that it was beyond his capacity to relieve Lucknow. Once more he withdrew to Mangalwar.

Meantime, the construction of a bridge of boats across the Ganges at Cawnpore had been proceeding. This was completed on 11 August. On the same day a message from Neill reported a rebel force to be collecting at Bithur (on the road leading from Cawnpore to Delhi) and threatening Cawnpore.

Havelock at once sent his sick and wounded and baggage across the river to Neill's entrenched camp; but, before moving there with his fighting troops, he determined to strike another blow at the rebels in his vicinity. That evening, therefore, Havelock once more advanced towards Lucknow. Three miles from Mangalwar he drove some hostile advanced troops out of a village and bivouacked for the night. Next morning, 12 August, he pushed on and for the third time drove the enemy out of Bashiratgani. British casualties during the day totalled thirty-five, including four in the Ferozepore Regiment. In the evening Havelock retired to Mangalwar. Next day, in torrents of rain, the British force crossed the bridge of boats and joined Neill. The bridge was then broken up, and the boats and rafts of which it was composed were laid up on the Cawnpore bank.

The situation at Cawnpore was not pleasant. Sickness was rife and nearly one-fifth of the British ranks were unfit for duty. However, Havelock determined to deal with the rebel force at Bithur without delay. He did so on 16 August, moving out from Cawnpore with a column of seven hundred and fifty British and two hundred and fifty Sikhs. The enemy fought with some obstinacy, but was nevertheless defeated and ejected from Bithur with heavy loss. Our casualties in action totalled forty-nine including seven of the Ferozepore Regiment. Brasyer had his horse shot under him whilst leading his men. After the fight was over, Havelock withdrew his column to Cawnpore.

It was on the day following the fight at Bithur that Havelock issued the Order of the Day from which is taken the quotation inscribed on his statue in Trafalgar Square:

> Soldiers your labours, your privations, your sufferings and your valour will not be forgotten by a grateful Country.

For the next month Havelock remained at Cawnpore awaiting reinforcements. He was unmolested by the enemy, and the health of his white troops gradually improved. For the greater part of this time Brasyer, with the Ferozepore Regiment, was absent from Cawnpore. They escorted a large convoy of sick and wounded to Allahabad, returning to rejoin Havelock after completion of this duty.

It will be remembered that a detachment of the Ferozepore Regiment, under Lieutenant Montagu, had been left behind as part of the garrison of Allahabad. This detachment was constantly in action with rebel parties in the neighbourhood and did good service. In September it was reduced to a strength of about one hundred and twenty, as General Sir James Outram took the remainder of the men with him when he passed through Allahabad with reinforcements on his way to join Havelock at Cawnpore.

Outram reached Cawnpore on 15 September. Though senior, he temporarily waived his rank so as to allow Havelock the honour of relieving Lucknow and accompanied the relief force in his civil capacity as Chief Commissioner of Oudh. Excluding the garrison that was to remain at Cawnpore, the force now assembled under Havelock totalled just over three thousand troops. The infantry were distributed in two brigades, under Brigadier-Generals Neill and Hamilton respectively, the Ferozepore Regiment being in the 2nd Brigade.[2]

---

[2] 1st Brigade – 5th Fusiliers, 84th Foot (with a detachment of the 64th attached), and 1st Madras Fusiliers.
2nd Brigade – 78th Highlanders, 90th Light Infantry and Regiment of Ferozepore.

Brasyer and his Sikhs were deputed to hold a position on the far bank of the Ganges to cover work on the reconstruction of the bridge of boats. Although the enemy was in close touch, he made no real attempt to hinder the passage of the river. The bridge was ready for use by 19 September, and during that day and the next Havelock's force filed across and concentrated on the far side.

HAVELOCK's ADVANCE ON LUCKNOW

The advance on Lucknow started on 21 September, in pouring rain. Opposition was soon encountered near Mangalwar. Havelock turned the hostile right flank and drove the rebels back with little difficulty. The British flank attack was carried out with great dash by the 90th Light Infantry and Ferozepore Regiment; our casualties were trifling. The force marched on and covered fourteen miles during the day.

On the 22nd the advance was continued unopposed for another twenty miles. The wet weather caused much discomfort.

After marching twelve miles on 23 September, Havelock found the enemy holding in strength a position near the Alambagh. Manoeuvre was rendered difficult by the flooded state of the country, but once more the hostile flank was turned and the rebels driven back with loss. Our casualties were only slight

Havelock halted on the 24th at the Alambagh whilst the enemy's position at Lucknow was reconnoitred. The city lay two miles ahead, to the north-east, on the far side of a broad canal spanned by the Charbagh Bridge. From this bridge the direct route to the Residency ran straight ahead, passing through the heart of the city. The Residency was situated just beyond the city limits on its north-eastern side, and backed on to the Gumti River. The plan decided upon was, first, to seize the Charbagh Bridge; then, to turn to the right along a road under the walls of the city on the northern edge of the canal; and finally, half-circling to the left, to approach the Residency from the south-east. By this means it was hoped to avoid street fighting as far as was possible.

Our object being to extricate the inmates of the Residency, the relieving force was to advance with a minimum of impedimenta. The sick and wounded, heavy baggage and large supply train which included over four thousand followers and an enormous number of cattle were to be left at the Alambagh. For their protection was detailed a force of three hundred men, drawn from various units and including about fifty of the Ferozepore Regiment.

FIRST RELIEF OF LUCKNOW, 25 September 1857

The morning of 25 September was fine and cool. Soon after 8 a.m. the advance from the Alambagh began. The 1st Brigade led the way, with a battery of guns well forward. The enemy defended the Charbagh Bridge with considerable obstinacy, and some little time elapsed before it was seized and made good. Havelock then moved off to the right along the edge of the canal leaving the 78th Highlanders and Ferozepore Regiment at the bridge to cover the movement and finally to follow in the rear.

The route taken by Havelock evidently came as a surprise to the rebels, for he met no serious opposition until he arrived in the area of palaces a short distance to the south-east of the Residency enclosure. Meanwhile, the Highlanders and the Sikhs at the Charbagh Bridge were somewhat heavily engaged. After three hours fighting there, they moved off up the road taken by the main British column. But by this time they had lost touch with it. As a result, they turned off to their left a mile short of the correct point. The mistake, however, proved fortunate; for they suddenly came upon the rear of some guns that were holding up Havelock's advance and rushed them without ceremony. The British force was now re-united, the 78th and Ferozepore Regiment becoming the head of the column instead of bringing up the rear.

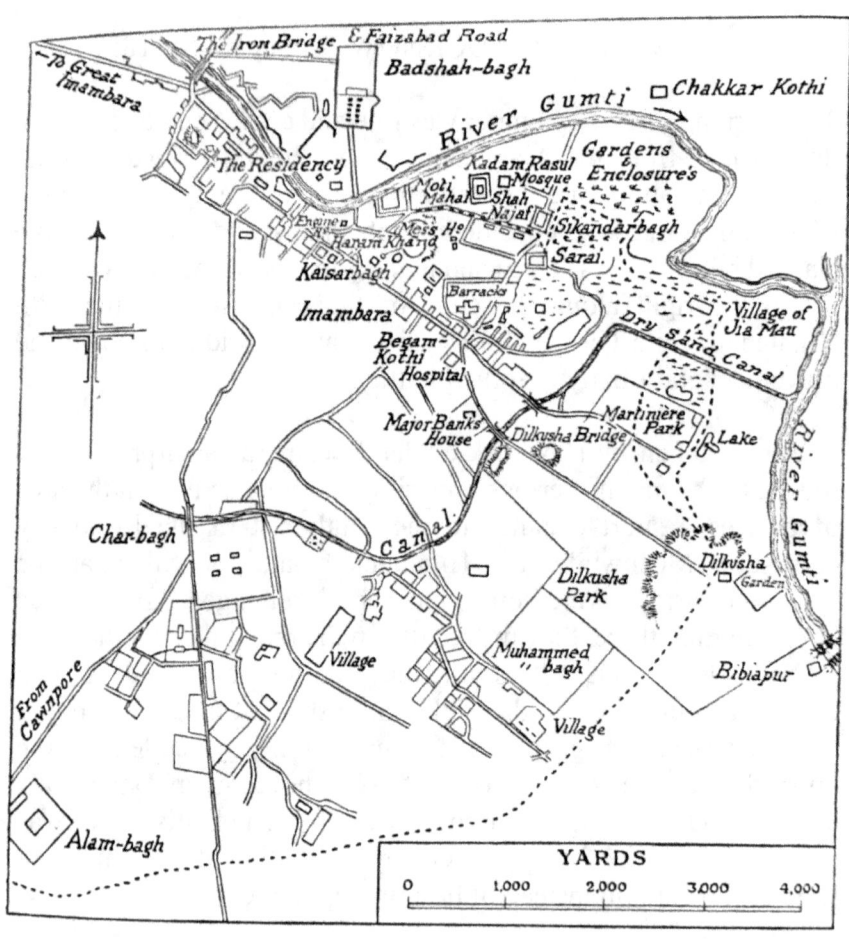

LUCKNOW. 1857–1858.

By this time it was dusk. The column was strung out over a considerable distance. The Residency was only about five hundred yards away, but the direct route ran up a narrow street defended by the enemy. Outram suggested halting awhile and closing up before making the final dash. Havelock, however, decided to reach the Residency without delay.

The Highlanders and Sikhs were called upon to lead the way. Led by Havelock and Outram in person, the two units moved forward. The 78th were in front, but the Sikhs followed eagerly and were soon mixed up with the Scots. The troops had to run a gauntlet of fire from the flat-roofed buildings on either side of the street, which itself was impeded with obstacles. But they fought their way through, and the Residency was gained. Brasyer claims to have been the first man to enter. A portion of Havelock's force did not reach the Residency enclosure that night, and it was not until the morning of 27 September that the whole column was within the defences.

The casualties incurred by the relief column on 25 and 26 September totalled five hundred and thirty-five –nearly one-quarter of the strength engaged. The tail of the column suffered considerable loss on the 26th. The losses of the Ferozepore Regiment amounted to forty-four, out of a strength of about three hundred and forty. Brasyer had two horses shot under him, but escaped unhurt himself.

As a reward for their conduct, Havelock promoted every Indian in the Ferozepore Regiment a step in rank, the subadars in lieu of promotion being awarded the 1st Class Indian Order of Merit.

DEFENCE OF LUCKNOW

After arriving within the Residency area, Outram took over from Havelock the command of the British forces. The original intention of withdrawing the inmates of the Residency from Lucknow was found to be impracticable. With an increase of over two thousand troops there was no longer any imminent danger of the garrison being overwhelmed, but none the less Outram had now to stand on the defensive and await relief in his turn. The rebels had been outwitted on 25 September, but they had not been decisively defeated. They still occupied the city in great strength and showed a bold spirit. The total number of sick, wounded, women and children with Outram amounted to one thousand five hundred, and the available transport was quite insufficient to remove them, even if it had been considered feasible to do so with any prospect of getting through the enemy without prohibitive loss.

With the increase of troops the circuit of the British position had to be enlarged, and on 27 September three palaces and their enclosures adjoining the Residency were occupied. For the next week or so, a number of sorties were made in order to improve the position. Thereafter, attack and defence were mainly confined to mining and countermining activities. Lieutenant W. Cross of the Ferozepore Regiment was wounded in a sortie on 6 October.

Outram defended his position for eight weeks before being relieved. His force was organised in two subordinate commands, Brigadier Inglis commanded the troops within the Residency enclosure and Havelock those, including the Regiment of Ferozepore, in the area adjoining it. It may here be noted that the Sikhs always designated not only the Residency enclosure but also the whole area defended by Outram at Lucknow as the 'Bailey Guard.' A reference by Indians to the defence of the 'Bailey Guard' therefore, must not necessarily be taken as applying merely to the local defence of the Bailey Guard gate of the Residency.

Outram's force was given no rest by the enemy and had always to be on the alert. Duties were constant and arduous. Rations were scanty throughout. Strange to say, the small detachment left at Alambagh on 25 September was never seriously threatened by the rebels and maintained its position without difficulty.

The casualties in Outram's force from 27 September to the date of the second relief of Lucknow were five hundred and fifty-one in all, but the losses of the Ferozepore Regiment during that period cannot be traced. Sergeant Major J. Brown was one of those killed.

The following are extracts from Outram's despatch, dealing with his defence:

> The Sikhs of the Ferozepore Regiment have zealously laboured at their own mines and, though separated only by a narrow passage sixteen feet wide from the enemy, have defended and protected their position. Captain Brasyer, commanding the Regiment of Ferozepore, and Captain Lockhart, commanding H.M. 78th Highlanders, have each maintained a difficult position with the most perfect success. These officers have gallantly led their men in every sortie.

SECOND RELIEF OF LUCKNOW, 17 November 1857

A relieving force under General Sir Colin Campbell, Commander-in-Chief in India, effected a junction with Outram on 17 November 1857. It was necessary for Campbell to return as quickly as he could to Cawnpore, where the situation was somewhat critical. He therefore decided to postpone to a later date his final settlement with the rebels at Lucknow. On the night of 22 November the whole of the British forces, including the women and children, were withdrawn from the Residency and from Lucknow. The operation was skilfully planned and executed. The enemy was taken by surprise, and the British retreat to the Alambagh was entirely unmolested. From the Alambagh Sir Colin Campbell started on the 27th for Cawnpore.

OUTRAM AT THE ALAMBAGH

Outram was left with a force of four thousand men and twenty-two guns to hold a position about the Alambagh in observation of the enemy at Lucknow – a bold gesture in face of rebel strength in the city amounting to over one hundred thousand. The Ferozepore Regiment was included in Outram's force: the strength of the

Battalion at this time was four British and two hundred and ninety-five Indian ranks.[3]

The position taken up by Outram was widely extended, and his defensive works occupied a circuit of about eleven miles. The force remained there for three months. Duties were arduous and harassing. The enemy kept constant touch, and there were almost daily skirmishes and minor encounters. Communication was maintained with Cawnpore, and the need for escorting convoys to that place, and back, reduced Outram's strength available for action considerably.

The enemy delivered a number of attacks, but they were all beaten off with but slight loss on the British side. In the affair of Guilee, on 22 December 1857, Outram took the offensive. Reporting on this action, Outram wrote that his "right column consisting of detachments of the 78th and 90th Regiments and of the Ferozepore Regiment of Sikhs, excited his admiration by the gallant way in which, with a cheer, they dashed at a strong position held by the enemy, and from which they were met by a heavy fire. Regardless of the overwhelming numbers and six guns reported to be posted there, the suddenness of the attack and the spirited way in which it was executed resulted in the immediate flight of the enemy, with hardly a casualty on our side."

FINAL OPERATIONS AT LUCKNOW, March 1858

At the beginning of March 1858, Sir Colin Campbell, with a large force, well equipped and accompanied by a siege train joined hands with Outram and started his methodical operations against Lucknow. By 5 March the force totalled over twenty-five thousand men with one hundred and sixty-four guns – the largest British army that had every taken the field in India.

---

[3] The other battalions in Outram's force were the 5th Fusiliers, 75th Foot, 78th Highlanders, 84th Foot, 90th Light Infantry, 1st Madras Fusiliers and 27th Madras Native Infantry. All units were below strength, the strongest being the 90th Light Infantry with five hundred and ninety effectives.

The Ferozepore Regiment – only three hundred and twenty Indian ranks strong, with three British officers (including the medical officer) – formed part of Outram's 1st Division and remained at Alambagh until 11 March. The Regiment was in action with the enemy on the 12th and 13th, but did not come in for severe fighting until the 14th. It was on this occasion included in the 4th Infantry Division under general Franks.

On 14 March the Ferozepore Regiment accompanied by sappers led the attack on the buildings and enclosure known as Little Imambara. One hundred Sikhs under Captain L. G. da Costa, with two companies of the 10th Foot, formed a storming party to assail two breaches that had been made in the walls; whilst Brasyer (now a major) with one hundred more Sikhs worked with a sapper party through some houses on a flank of the breach. Having no other British combatant officer available, Brasyer placed the Colours and the remainder of his men in charge of the doctor, Surgeon J. Browne, with orders to keep as close to him as possible. These orders were faithfully executed.

Brasyer's movement, thanks to effective demolition work by the sappers, was quickly successful and distracted the enemy's attention from the breaches just as our storming party made their assault. The Little Imambara was speedily captured with unexpected ease. The Colours of the Ferozepore regiment were planted over the gateway and the appointed task for the day was completed.

But the Sikhs were eager to follow up their success. With the acquiescence of general Franks, they dashed under Brasyer and effected an entrance into Kaiserbagh palace enclosure – the citadel of the enemy's position in Lucknow. Here the enemy was present in strength, and there was a temporary check. But supports of the 10th and 90th Regiments came up, followed quickly by further reinforcements. Before long the whole of the Kaiserbagh was in British hands. Brasyer, personally, pushed the Regimental Colour of the Ferozepore Regiment through a gun-shot hole in the highest dome of the palace as a signal to our artillery that the place was ours. The casualties of the Regiment this day totalled forty-two –

the highest number incurred by any unit. Captain da Costa was among those killed.

On 16 March the Ferozepore Regiment formed part of a force under Outram which regained possession of the Residency. Brasyer was severely wounded, but remained at duty and continued to command his regiment, although he had to be carried about in a litter for some time.

The enemy was completely defeated and dispersed by 21 March, and Sir C. Campbell's operations at Lucknow came to an end. The total casualties in his force between 2 and 21 March were seven hundred and thirty-five. Those of the Ferozepore Regiment during this period numbered fifty-seven, not a large figure according to the standards of the Great War of 1914–1919. But this was much the highest percentage of losses incurred by any unit of the force, and in actual figures second only to the seventy-six casualties of the 93rd Highlanders, a battalion numerically three times as strong.

After the capture of Lucknow, major operations came to an end so far as the Regiment of Ferozepore was concerned. For more than a year longer, however, the Regiment remained in Oudh. It formed part of various small columns engaged in pacifying the country and rounding up parties of rebels, and took part in a number of minor encounters. Lieutenant Montagu and the detachment at Allahabad rejoined battalion headquarters during this period.

Operations came to an end in June 1859, when the Regiment marched off to be quartered at Ferozepore; it arrived there on 7 September 1859.

The services of the Regiment in the Indian Mutiny were commemorated on its Colours by the inscription: 'LUCKNOW, Defence and Capture.' The staff of one of the Colours was broken by a gun-shot during the operations at Lucknow. It was repaired and is still doing duty with the Regiment, though the Colour attached to it has been renewed.

Brasyer, who commanded throughout the Mutiny period was constantly commended in despatches, both for gallantry and leadership. In the words of Outram, Brasyer 'always distinguished himself most highly in command of his Regiment.' Starting the campaign as a lieutenant, he finished it as a Lieutenant Colonel and a Companion of the Order of the Bath.

Only five British combatant officers served with the Battalion between 1857 and 1859; of these, one was killed and three wounded. The British sergeant major was killed at Lucknow and his successor wounded. The British quartermaster sergeant remained at Allahabad in charge of the regimental stores and escaped unhurt.

As a special mark of distinction for its conduct during the Mutiny, the Ferozepore Regiment was granted the privilege of wearing a red pugaree as its headdress.

CHAPTER 2
1859–1893

OPERATIONS ON THE NORTH-WEST FRONTIER

The Battalion remained at Ferozepore but a short time. In February 1860 it marched off to Sialkot to form part of the Viceroy's escort during a big Durbar. From Sialkot it accompanied the Viceroy to Kalka, thence returned to Ferozepore and after a few days was on the road again for Sialkot, which was to be its new station. Sialkot was reached on 4 May. There were no quarters available, and the Regiment for a considerable time was employed in the construction of buildings for itself to occupy.

Lieutenant Colonel Brasyer vacated command during 1860 and was succeeded by Captain A. W. Montagu. In June 1861 the Battalion moved to Peshawar. In the same month Major C. C. G. Ross was appointed commandant; he was destined to hold command for no less than fourteen years.

The reorganisation of the Army in India after the Indian Mutiny began to take shape in 1861. The Honourable East India Company having ceased to exist, all its troops had become part of Her Majesty's Forces. The three Presidency armies remained as separate entities, but now included Indian troops only. In the Bengal Army irregular regiments were absorbed into the Line as regulars and received new designations. For a few months the Regiment of Ferozepore was numbered 15th. It then received the official title of 14th Regiment of Bengal Native Infantry, but became known generally as the 14th Sikhs.

The organisation of the Indian single battalion infantry regiment was modelled on the old irregular system. The establishment of British officers was brought down to the meagre figure previously allotted to irregular units. British non-commissioned ranks were abolished. The strength of Indian ranks was laid down as sixteen Indian officers and six hundred and ninety-six other ranks, organised in eight companies.

THE AMBELA EXPEDITION, 1863

Towards the end of 1863 came the Ambela campaign, in the course of which there was some severe fighting. The object of the expedition was to break up the settlement of Hindustani fanatics at Malka, on the northern face of the Mahaban Mountain. For some time these men had been a chronic cause of disturbance in that part of the North-West Frontier.

The British plan was to advance on Malka via the Ambela Pass[4] and Chamla valley. A force about six thousand strong was assembled under the command of Brigadier General Sir Neville Chamberlain, who gained the summit of the Ambela Pass on 20 October almost unopposed. The 14th Sikhs were not included in the original expeditionary force.

After reaching the head of the Ambela Pass, Chamberlain was confronted quite unexpectedly by a new situation, for the Bunerwal tribe rose against us. With the warlike Bunerwals menacing our left flank, an advance through the Chamla valley on Malka would be a risky operation. Chamberlain therefore decided to take up a defensive position on the summit of the Ambela Pass, while awaiting reinforcements, and to allow the tribal combination to break their strength against it.

---

[4]Also known as the Panidara or Sarkhawai Pass

Bunerwals and Hindustani fanatics delivered a violent attack on 26 October. They were repulsed with loss, though not without some stiff fighting. Next day the enemy was joined by large reinforcements from Swat, Bajaur and elsewhere, and it became clear that we had to face a general combination of tribes from the Indus to the Afghan border. The number of men under arms against us was computed at not less than fifteen thousand.

The 14th Sikhs – the first of the reinforcements to reach Sir N. Chamberlain–arrived at the Ambela camp on 27 October, under the command of Major Ross.

The British camp was located near the summit of the pass, which runs roughly from west to east. The heights commanding the camp on all sides, but especially from the north, east and west, were held by strong infantry piquets. These posts were protected by stone walls and abattis; but the ground was extremely broken and much wooded, and the enemy was able to mass unseen close by in large numbers. It must be remembered too, that the power of our firearms was not comparable with what it is to-day. The Indian troops were still armed with the old smooth-bore musket, though the British infantry had Enfield rifles.

On 30 October the Crag Piquet, an important post to the south-east of the camp, was captured by the enemy. It was retaken the same day. The 14th Sikhs were not engaged.

There was some severe fighting on 6 November, when detachments covering the withdrawal of parties working on a new road were attacked with great boldness; but again the 14th Sikhs were not one of the units engaged.

On the night of 12 November the enemy attacked the Crag Piquet in strength and with great fury. The piquet had been enlarged and strengthened since 30 October; it was on this occasion commanded by Major Brownlow, who had under him one hundred and fifteen men of his own Regiment (the 20th Punjabis), thirty men of the 14th Sikhs and fifteen of the 101st Royal Bengal Fusiliers. From 10p.m. onwards the tribesmen delivered repeated attacks with the utmost bravery; all were repulsed, though not without difficulty. The enemy withdrew about 4 a.m., having suffered severe losses.

At 8 a.m. on 13 November, Major Brownlow and his men were relieved by a detachment of the 1st Punjab Infantry under Lieutenant Davidson, who had also with him a small party of the 14th Sikhs. Scarcely had the relief been effected when the post was again attacked in great force. Davidson was killed and his men were driven out in confusion. The small detachment of the 14th posted in the lower portion of the piquet was suddenly overwhelmed by the rush of fugitives from above, and practically the whole party perished. Among those killed was Subadar Jowahir Shah, who had been awarded the Indian Order of Merit for gallantry at Lucknow in 1857.

Major Ross of the 14th Sikhs happened to be the officer in command of the advanced piquets that day. He was in the British camp when the sudden fall of the Crag Piquet took place. The sight of our men retiring rapidly down the hill caused some temporary confusion in the camp. Major Ross, however quickly assembled all available men of the 14th, together with parties of other units, and advanced up the hill towards the Crag Piquet. He was not strong enough to attempt its recapture at once, but proceeding half-way up the hill, he opened fire to engage the enemy's attention pending the arrival of reinforcements. These arrived shortly, in the shape of a British battalion – the 101st Fusiliers. With them Ross advanced and the Crag Piquet was retaken. Our total casualties during the day were considerable (one hundred and fifty-eight in all).

On the morning of 18 November the position of the British camp was changed, being moved from the vicinity of the road to the heights on the south of the pass. Our piquets on the left, or northern, flank were withdrawn from the Guru Mountain. The retirement was effected without difficulty, the British movement evidently taking the enemy unawares. But before long the tribesmen, supposing that our withdrawal had been made as a preliminary to a general retreat, advanced in great strength and attacked furiously the new British left flank.

Our defences here were small breastworks on the side of the hill held temporarily to prevent the enemy pressing upon the British camp before the troops were thoroughly established in their new positions. The posts were not strong, they were rather advanced, exposed to flank attack and in fact not easily defensible. They were held by one hundred and thirty men of the 14th Sikhs under Major Ross, who had orders to maintain his position until dark.

The enemy's attack began at about 11a.m. The 14th were very hard pressed and distinguished themselves greatly by the tenacity of their defence. Portions of the line were forced back by sheer weight of numbers; but reinforcements, amounting eventually to seven companies of various battalions, gradually arrived and the line was restored. At the close of day the enemy retired, having suffered heavily. The total British losses amounted to one hundred and eighteen. Out of the one hundred and thirty men of the 14th Sikhs there were seventy-two casualties; Lieutenant W.F. Mosley was killed and Lieutenant A. D. C. Inglis wounded. For their gallantry in action this day Subadar Major Sekundar Khan and twelve Indian other ranks were awarded the Indian Order of Merit.

The Battalion was not seriously in action again after 18 November. On the 20th the Crag Piquet for the third time was lost and recaptured, but the 14th were not engaged. After this date the enemy made no further attack in force and his gatherings dwindled away. In December, British reinforcements arrived. General Garvock, who had succeeded Sir N. Chamberlain in command of the force owing to the latter having been wounded, took the offensive on 17 December. Malka was destroyed on the 22nd. The expedition came to an end and the British force withdrew to the Peshawar valley. The 14th Sikhs marched into Peshawar on 31 December.

1864–1877

They remained there only a few days before moving off to their new station, Mian Mir (Lahore Cantonment), where they arrived in February 1864.

The next twelve years were peaceful. The Regiment was stationed at Mian Mir for one year only. From January 1863 till January 1868 it was quartered at Benares. Thence it moved to Fort William, Calcutta. In June 1869 it was transferred to Alipore, but only remained there seven months before being moved to Jullundur. From Jullundur the Regiment went to Rawalpindi in April 1872, and at the end of 1875 it was transferred to Peshawar. Throughout this period of twelve years the 14th were commanded by Colonel Ross, who was succeeded on 1 September 1875 by Major L. H. Williams.

In 1864 a new scheme for the class composition of Bengal regiments was brought into force. That of the 14th, however, remained unchanged. The Regiment continued to consist principally of cis-Sutlej Sikhs, with a small admixture of trans-Sutlej Sikhs and Punjabi Mahommedans. The Subadar Major from 1863 to 1871 was a Punjabi Mahommedan, Sekundar Khan, who has already been mentioned. By 1870 we find that a few Pathans had been introduced into the Regiment, owing to their utility as interpreters on the North-West Frontier.

There was no change between 1861 and 1875 in the establishment of Indian ranks, but that of the British officers was slightly increased. By 1870 these totalled eight and consisted of the commandant, two wing commanders, four wing officers (including the adjutant and quartermaster) and a medical officer,

As for the armament the Regiment was re-armed with Enfield rifles in 1872 and with Snider rifles in 1875.

The official title of the Regiment was slightly amended in 1856 to be the 14th (Ferozepore) Regiment of Bengal Native Infantry.

THE JOWAKI EXPEDITION, 1877–1878

In the autumn of 1877 punitive operations were undertaken against the Jowaki Afridis. Two columns were formed to enter the Jowaki hills, one from Kohat and the other from the Peshawar side. The Peshawar column, under Brigadier General Ross who had held command of the 14th Sikhs from 1861 to 1875 was divided into two brigades. The 14th Sikhs (489 rifles strong) formed part of the 2nd Brigade under Colonel H. J. Buchanan, together with three hundred rifles of the 9th Foot and the 20th Punjabis (360 rifles).

The Kohat column entered the Jowaki country in November, but the Peshawar column did not advance until 4 December. It is unnecessary to describe the operations in detail. The enemy made little resistance and the fighting was not severe, though there were always difficulties of ground to be surmounted. British columns moved all over the country and various villages were destroyed. The troops were withdrawn at the end of January 1878. Our total casualties during the operations amounted to sixty-two, of which sixteen were incurred by the 14th Sikhs.

THE SECOND AFGHAN WAR, 1878

More serious was the Second Afghan War, which broke out in the autumn of 1878.

In order to invade Afghanistan by the Khyber route, the 1st Division was assembled at Jamrud under the Command of Lieutenant General Sir Sam Browne. Four infantry brigades, each of three battalions, were included in the division. The 14th Sikhs, together with the 81st Foot and 27th Punjabis, formed the 3rd Brigade under Brigadier General Appleyard. The Battalion, commanded by Lieutenant Colonel Williams, took the field with a strength of seven British officers and six hundred and seven Indian ranks.

General Browne's first task was to clear the Khyber Pass of the enemy. The Afghans were known to be holding a position at Ai Masjid, and it was estimated that their strength was about four thousand with some guns. The local frontier tribesmen were not involved in hostilities against us.

ALI MASJID, 21 November 1878

Sir S. Browne decided to combine a frontal attack against the Ali Masjid position with movements against the hostile left flank and rear. Accordingly, the 1st and 2nd Brigades marched off during the night of 20 November to carry out the encircling movements; but, for various reasons, they did not reach their allotted positions by the time that it had been arranged for the frontal attack to begin. The remainder of the 1st Division, two infantry brigades, a cavalry brigade and artillery, started from Jamrud at 7 a.m. on 21 November to advance into the Khyber Pass. Four companies of the 14th Sikhs headed the advanced guard, which marched in the following order:

> Two hundred and fifty men (four companies), 14th Sikhs.
> Two hundred and fifty men, 81st Foot.
> 2nd and 3rd Companies, Sappers and Miners.
> Forty sabres, 10th Hussars.
> One battery, Royal Horse Artillery.
> One mountain battery.
> Remainder of the 14th Sikhs.

There was a possibility that the enemy might offer opposition at the Shahgai ridge, some two and a half miles short of Ali Masjid fort. This, however, was not the case, and the head of the advanced guard occupied the ridge at about 11 a.m. The main column closed up and arrangements were made for the further advance.

One of the difficulties of mountain warfare – that of keeping units concentrated and avoiding undue dispersion–soon began to be in evidence in 3rd Brigade. Protective detachments were sent out to either flank; other detachments were pushed forward to cover sapper parties engaged in improving the road; and the brigade became much scattered.

The Khyber Pass in the vicinity of Ali Masjid runs roughly from south to north. The Ali Masjid fort, situated on a detached hill rising precipitately some four hundred feet from the trough of the pass on the right bank of the Khyber River, formed the centre of the Afghan position, which lay astride the Khyber gorge. The enemy also held an advanced line of entrenchments on a ridge west of the river about half a mile south of the fort.

At midday, Afghan guns opened fire, but with no appreciable effect.

It had been planned that the frontal attack of the British main column should start at 1 p.m., by which time the two brigades carrying out the movements against the enemy's left flank and rear should have reached their allotted positions. Time went on. however, without any sign of the turning columns, and at 2:30 p.m. Sir S. Browne issued orders for the attack to begin. The 4th Brigade, forming the Right Attack, was to advance on the east of the road; the 3rd Brigade, forming the Left Attack, was to descend from the Shahgai ridge, cross the Khyber River at Lala China and then advance northwards against the enemy's advanced position. To reach this, about two miles of difficult ground had to be traversed.

So many detachments had been made for various duties that there remained available in the 3rd Brigade to carry out the attack only one Company of the 14th Sikhs, two of the 27th Punjabis and five companies of the 81st Foot. The advance was led by Captain J. G. Maclean with the 14th Sikhs' company, half deployed in a skirmishing line and half in support. The two Punjabi companies followed, with the 81st farther back in reserve.

Progress, though slow, was steady. By 5p.m. Captain Maclean was at close grips with the enemy and under sharp fire, both frontal and enfilade. The Sikh Company was all in the firing line, with the Punjabis in close support. Now, however, orders were received to retire. There being still no sign of the British turning columns Sir S. Browne had decided to break off his attack so as to avoid unnecessary casualties. The withdrawal from close contact with the enemy was not an easy operation. Encouraged by our retirement, the Afghans' fire became more accurate; and before the Sikhs and Punjabis could retreat out of range considerably more casualties were inflicted on them than during their advance. The men of the 14th behaved very well, and no less than eight of the company were later awarded the Indian Order of Merit for gallantry. Captain

Maclean was wounded, and of the Indian ranks eight were killed and sixteen wounded out of a strength in action not exceeding sixty-five.

The British force bivouacked for the night in readiness to renew the attack next morning. At daybreak on 22 November, however, it was found that the Afghans – having become aware of the threat to their flank and rear – had retreated hurriedly up the pass, abandoning twenty-four guns.

The British casualties at Ali Masjid on 21 November were only fifty, all told. Of this total the 14th Sikhs, as already stated, incurred twenty-five. The 27th Punjabis lost twelve, including two British officers killed.

The main column remained halted at Ali Masjid on the 22nd. Next day General Browne, with his headquarters, the 10th Hussars, Guides Cavalry, a horse artillery battery and the 14th Sikhs, marched on to Landi Khana. On the 24th the bulk of the 1st Division was concentrated at Dakka, at the western end of the Khyber Pass, and remained there for several weeks. No further opposition had been encountered.

On 27 November the 14th were ordered to take up their quarters in the Afghan barracks at Dakka. These barracks were in an indescribably filthy state, but they were cleaned out as thoroughly as possible before being occupied. Tents and bedding for the Battalion came up on the 30th, but their insanitary surroundings had already infected the men. On 2 December an epidemic of 'typho-malarial fever' broke out.

Six men died that day and several more the next. On the 8th the Battalion was moved into camp two miles away, but the sickness went on and men died daily. Finally, on 13 December, the 14th were ordered back to Peshawar, where they arrived four days later. Twenty-seven sick men were left behind at Dakka of whom only nine survived. This ended the brief participation of the Battalion in the Second Afghan War.

The epidemic continued to rage at Peshawar, and the Regiment was sent off to march by easy stages to Ambala. It reached that place on 2 February 1879. Before it was stamped out, the epidemic cost the Regiment over two hundred casualties.

WAZIRISTAN EXPEDITION, 1881

The 14th remained quietly at Ambala till 1881 when they returned to the frontier to take part in a punitive expedition into Waziristan. The Battalion reached Rawalpindi on 17 April, travelling by train. Next day it started to march to Bannu, where it arrived on the 28th, having covered one hundred and ninety-two miles in eleven days in considerable heat. At Bannu it joined the column assembled under Brigadier General J. J. H. Gordon. Another column, assembled at Tank, had by this time already advanced into Wazir country.

The Bannu column[5] moved forward into hostile territory on 2 May and, proceeding by the Khaisora valley, reached Razmak on the 9th. There it got into communication with the Tank column at Makin. The enemy offered little resistance and soon submitted to terms. General Gordon's column was back in Bannu by 22 May, and the expeditionary force was broken up. The total British casualties amounted to only thirty-two. Although the losses were trifling, there was nevertheless the usual amount of arduous duty involved in a frontier expedition, and the heat was very trying.

Before reaching Bannu, Subadar Major Didar Singh of the 14th Sikhs died on 20 May. He was a splendid soldier and had held office as Subadar Major for ten years. He had served in the Regiment since 1854 and had received his first promotion for good service at Lucknow in 1857.

---

[5] It consisted of eight mountain guns, 18th Bengal Cavalry, No 6 Company Sappers and Miners, 4th Rifle brigade, 14th Sikhs, 20th, 21st and 30th Punjabis, and the 5th Punjab infantry.

The Regiment began its return march from Bannu on 25 May in intense heat, reached Khushalgarh on 4 June and travelling thence by train, arrived back at Ambala on 8 June.

1881–1888

In October 1881 the 14th Sikhs moved from Ambala to Agra. There they remained till December 1884, when they marched in relief to Jhelum, and Jhelum was the regimental station for the next five years.

In May 1884, Colonel Williams was succeeded as commandant by Colonel G. N. Channer, V.C., who held that appointment till September 1888; his successor was Lieutenant Colonel W. V. Ellis.

The Battalion went to Rawalpindi in March 1885 to join the Durbar Camp held there by the Viceroy (Lord Dufferin) for the reception of the Amir of Afghanistan. In April, when war with Russia appeared imminent, the 14th Sikhs were warned to be in readiness for service as part of the I Army Corps.

The Regiment was absent from Jhelum for most of the cold weather season, 1885–1886, taking part in a camp of exercise at Delhi and marching to and from that place.

Some important changes in the organisation of infantry regiments of the Bengal Army were made between 1882 and 1888. These were, no doubt, partially due to the experiences of the Second Afghan War and to the threat of war with Russia in 1885, when it was realised that the organisation of the Indian infantry did not meet the requirements of war on a large scale.

The first change was made in 1882, when another officer was added to the establishment of British officers, and fifteen additional sepoys were allotted to each company. This caused the establishment to become 9 British officers (including the medical officer), 16 Indian officers and 816 Indian other ranks. Five years later the establishment of Indian other ranks was raised further to 896.

The bulk of the Indian infantry continued to be single battalion regiments, but in 1886 a system of linked battalions was introduced. Under this system, which lasted till 1922, battalions were linked together in groups – generally of three units – and allotted what was termed a regimental centre. Recruits enlisted in one battalion were liable for service with any other battalion of its group in the event of war. It was the intention that one battalion of the group should always be located at the regimental centre. The object of this scheme was that, in emergency, the unit at the regimental centre could be called upon to supply drafts for other units of the group. Although units were thus linked, in no sense did they become battalions of the same regiment; each single battalion regiment preserved its individual designation and identity, and when it went on active service provided its own depot at the regimental centre. The 14th were linked with the 15th and 45th Sikhs and Multan became the regimental centre.

In 1886, also a system of reserves was introduced. This comprised an "active reserve" composed of men transferred after not less than five or more than ten years colour service, and a garrison reserve of men pensioned after twenty-one years service, or who had a combined twenty-one years colour and reserve service.

A slight change to the official title of the Regiment was notified in 1885, when it became the 14th Regiment of Bengal Infantry (The Ferozepore Sikhs). This was modified a few years later to
14th (The Ferozepore Sikh) Regiment of Bengal Infantry.

An order was issued in 1883 amending the class composition of Indian units as laid down in 1864. The 14th Sikhs were now to consist of seven companies of Sikhs and one company of Punjabi Mahommedans. In 1885 instructions were received to allow the Moslem company to die out; and gradually the Regiment became, for the first time, a corps composed entirely of Sikhs. To meet the need for Pushtu-speaking interpreters when operating on the North-West Frontier, two Sikhs from trans-frontier districts were enlisted for each company.

BLACK MOUNTAIN EXPEDITION, 1888

In the autumn of 1888 the Hazara Field Force was formed to carry out punitive operations against tribes of the Black Mountain County, lying to the north-west of Abbottabad. The force roughly of the strength of a division was commanded by Major General J. W. McQueen. By 1 October it was concentrated at Oghi and Darband, and organised into four separate columns. The 14th Sikhs, Under Lieutenant Colonel W. V. Ellis formed part of Number 3 Column,[6] which with Numbers 1 and 2 Columns concentrated at Oghi.

Infantry battalions took the field six hundred strong. Only a light scale of transport was authorised; no tents were taken, all equipment and supplies beyond Oghi and Darband were carried on mules.

During the expedition no serious fighting fell to the lot of the 14th Sikhs. The three columns from Oghi on 4 October advanced up different spurs of the Black Mountain. No.3 Column, which was accompanied by General McQueen, met with no opposition, and all the columns reached their objectives without difficulty. Heavy rain fell during the night and caused considerable discomfort to the troops in bivouac.

Next day No.3 Column reached the crest of the main Black Mountain ridge, after brushing aside slight opposition. The 14th Sikhs had two men wounded.

On 6 October No.3 Column, headed by the 14th Sikhs, advanced towards the village of Seri. Owing to the difficulties of the track, which ran through thick forest and had to be improved by sappers and working parties nearly the whole way, progress was extremely slow. The enemy worried us by constant sniping, but did not appear in large numbers. The Sikhs, with General McQueen and his

---

[6] No.3 Column, under Lieutenant Colonel M. S. J. Sutherland, consisted of two guns each of the 3/1st South Irish Battery R.A. and the Derajat Mountain Battery, half No.3 Company Sappers and Miners, the 2nd Royal Sussex Regiment, 14th Sikhs and 24th Punjabis.

headquarter staff, reached the hamlet of Kaima at midday. Here it was decided to halt and bivouac for the night. Our casualties during the day totalled nine, of which five were incurred by the 14th.

Next day, as the water supply at Kaima was scanty and it would be difficult to move a large body of transport animals farther towards Seri till the route had been improved, General McQueen decided to return to the crest of the Black Mountain. The withdrawal of No.3 Column was covered by the 14th Sikhs as rearguard, and the Battalion lost three men killed and two wounded. The column bivouacked on the northern slopes of Akhund Baba.

After 7 October various small columns visited and destroyed a number of villages and desultory operations continued till the beginning of November. The 14th Sikhs, however, were not further engaged with the enemy. The Battalion was employed for a time in road-making, finally rejoining No.3 Column at Oghi on 6 November. The Field Force was broken up five days later.

The 14th Sikhs marched from Oghi on 13 November and arrived at Rawalpindi on the 21st; there they took part in a camp of exercise, and finally returned to Jhelum just before Christmas.

1889–1893

Five peaceful years followed. In 1889 the Regiment re-armed with Martini-Henry rifles. In 1890 it moved from Jhelum to Peshawar, and at the end of 1893 it marched in relief from Peshawar to Ferozepore.

CHAPTER 3
1894–1895

WAZIRISTAN AND CHITRAL

The 14th Sikhs arrived at Ferozepore from Peshawar on 19 January 1894. On the following 15 March new Colours were presented to the Regiment. On 15 June, A and B Companies proceeded to Gilgit to form the British Agent's escort. This detachment was commanded by Captain C. R. Ross, and included Lieutenants H. J. Jones and H. K. Harley with four Indian officers and two hundred and four other ranks. On arrival in the Gilgit area, A Company was sent to Mastuj whilst B Company remained at Gilgit.

WAZIRISTAN, 1894–1896

At the beginning of November 1894 the headquarters four hundred men of the Battalion left Ferozepore for garrison duty at Dera Ismail Khan. A month later they moved to Jandola, in order to hold that frontier post during the progress of the Waziristan campaign being conducted by General Sir William Lockhart. On 13 January 1895 the 14th Sikhs were attached to the 2nd Brigade of the Waziristan Field Force and advanced with that formation into the Khaisora valley. During this advance the Battalion was detached with a flying column under Colonel Gaselee to punish a certain section of the Mahsuds, and had two men wounded – the only casualties incurred by the 14th in the campaign. After being much employed on convoy duty, the Battalion returned to Jandola on 16 February.

The Waziristan Field Force was broken up on 31 March, but the 14th Sikhs were detailed to remain at Sarwekai, in Wazir territory. In December 1895 battalion headquarters moved to Ferozepore, but a detachment of three hundred men was left at Sarwekai and did not rejoin headquarters until the end of 1896.

CHITRAL 1895

Meanwhile there had been trouble in Chitral. On 1 January 1895 the Mehtar of Chitral was murdered. There ensued a state of unrest in the country pending a settlement of the problem of succession. At the time of the murder the British Political Agent in Gilgit (Surgeon-Major G. Robertson) was at Gilgit, his assistant, Lieutenant B. E. M. Gurdon, with an escort of nine Sikhs, happened to be on a visit to Chitral. A Company of the 14th Sikhs was at Mastuj, B Company at Gilgit.

The distance from Gilgit to Mastuj is one hundred and fifty-five miles, the route running through difficult mountainous country and crossing one pass over twelve thousand feet high. From Mastuj to Chitral is sixty-five miles. There was a party of Kashmir State troops at Mastuj and further detachments were stationed at various posts between Mastuj and Gilgit.

Immediately after the murder of the Chitral ruler, fifty men of A Company, 14th Sikhs, under Subadar Gurmukh Singh from Mastuj reinforced the small escort with Lieutenant Gurdon in Chitral, arriving there on 5 January; and, in anticipation of trouble, further Kashmir infantry were moved towards Mastuj. In the middle of January the British Agent started personally from Gilgit for Chitral to investigate the situation. From Mastuj he took with him Lieutenant Harley, the remainder of A Company 14th Sikhs, and about three hundred Kashmir infantry. He arrived at Chitral on

31 January and took possession of the fort as a precautionary measure. Gurdon had already collected a store of supplies there.

Meantime a Pathan firebrand, one Umra Khan of Bajaut, had invaded Chitral territory from the south with a considerable armed following. At first the Chitralis opposed him, but their resistance was feeble, and by the beginning of February Umra Khan was in possession of the fort of Drosh not far south of Chitral. At Drosh he was joined by a certain Sher Afzul and agreed to support the latter in his claim to become Mehtar of Chital. The first object of the two men was to get rid of the British from Chitral. Fruitless negotiations took place with the British Agent.

At the end of February the Chitralis, who were still holding position twelve miles south of Chitral, suddenly went over to what they deemed to be the stronger side. On 3 March, late in the afternoon, news reached Chitral fort that Sher Afzul was approaching with a large force of Pathans and Chitralis.

The garrison of the fort consisted of A Company, 14th Sikhs, under Lieutenant Harley (two Indian officers and ninety-nine other ranks), about three hundred men of the 4th Kashmir Rifles (Imperial Service Troops) with whom Captains Campbell, Townshend and Baird were doing duty as special service officers, and some Panyali and Hunza levies. The British Agent and his assistant were also present, while Surgeon-Captain Whitchurch was in medical charge. Captain C. P. Campbell was in command of the troops.

AFFAIR OF 3 MARCH, 1895

Campbell decided to move out at once and carry out what has been described as a reconnaissance in force. With him went two hundred men of the Kashmir Rifles and all the British officers except Lieutenant Harley, who was left in command of the fort. The enemy was encountered about two miles away holding a position in some villages. Campbell attacked. The enemy was in greater strength than had been anticipated; the Kashmir infantry were somewhat roughly handled; and a retirement on the fort had to be carried out by troops considerably demoralised in face of numerous and exultant tribesmen.

At about 6 p.m. Harley received a message instructing him to bring out a party of his men to cover the retreat. He at once proceeded with fifty rifles to take up a position in a *serai* a quarter of a mile away from the fort. The Sikhs were formed in line extended at three paces interval, kneeling, with bayonets fixed. By this time it was quite dark and most difficult to distinguish friend from foe. Absolutely cool and steady, the Sikhs remained at their posts till the whole of the retreating force had passed through them and were well on their way back to the fort. Harley then withdrew his men by alternate sections in perfect order, firing occasional volleys at the enemy. They were exposed to a heavy fire all the time, but were saved by the darkness from suffering any casualties. The fort was reached at about 7:30 p.m.

In this action of 3 March Captain Campbell was severely and Captain Baird mortally wounded, while the Kashmir troops lost fifty-six officers and men killed and wounded. Captain C. V. F. Townsend, later to be the defender of Kut, succeeded Campbell in command of the Chitral garrison. The fort now became closely invested.

MASTUJ

Before proceeding with the story of the siege, it will be more convenient to turn to events in the neighbourhood of Mastuj.

On 1 March a subadar and forty men of the Kashmir Rifles left Mastuj for Chitral with a consignment of ammunition. When he reached Buni, two stages (twenty-three miles) from Mastuj, the subadar found the road broken and heard rumours that he was to be attacked. He accordingly reported to Lieutenant F. J. Moberly, the special duty officer with the Kashmir troops in Mastuj, and asked for instructions. This report reached Mastuj on the evening of 4 March.

Meanwhile, on the 3rd, Captain Ross with B Company, 14th Sikhs, had arrived at Mastuj from Gilgit. After hearing of the report from Buni, Ross started at dusk on the 4th with fifty Sikhs to support the subadar there. Marching through the night, Ross on arrival at Buni

THE NORTH-WEST FRONTIER, INDIA.

next morning found everything quiet. He instructed the Kashmir subadar to await a party of Sappers and Miners, under Lieutenants Edwardes and Fowler, who were on their way to Chitral with engineering stores, before proceeding any farther. Ross then returned to Mastuj, which he reached after dark on the 5th, his party having marched forty-six miles in twenty-four hours.

The sapper detachment left Mastuj on 5 March, picked up the Kashmir party at Buni next day, and continued its march on Chitral. On the evening of the 6th there was a message from Lieutenant Edwardes, dated noon the same day, reporting a rumour that he was to be attacked near Reshun (thirteen miles beyond Buni).

Ross decided to move at once with his company to support Edwards and marched out of Mastuj on the morning of 7 March. With Ross were Lieutenant Jones, one Indian officer, ninety-three Indian other ranks, a hospital assistant and sixteen followers. Nine days rations and one hundred and forty rounds of ammunition per rifle were taken.

Buni was reached at 11 p.m. that night. Here the Indian officer and thirty-three men were left behind. Ross with the remainder started for Reshun the next morning, 8 March, taking three days' cooked rations and one hundred rounds per rifle.

DISASTER OF KORAGH DEFILE

Soon after 1 p.m. the party entered a narrow defile below the village of Koragh. The mountains here close in on the Mastuj River, which is throughout the defile a rapid and unfordable torrent. The track lay on the left bank. The defile is about half a mile long, and the mountain ridge rising abruptly above the path sloped down to the river in a succession of very steep spurs divided by stone shoots. At the Reshun, or lower, end of the defile the path ascended a steep spur.

Captain Ross had no knowledge of the turn of events at Chitral. At the same time he knew that the whole countryside was in a state of unrest; and he himself was advancing to the assistance of Edwardes's party, which was reported to be in danger of attack. It seems therefore distinctly rash to have entered the Koragh defile without, at any rate, first reconnoitring the heights above the path.

Probably, for the sake of speed, Ross decided to take the risk. The result was to be disastrous.

As the advanced party of Sikhs was ascending the spur at the lower end of the defile, it was fired upon from a *sangar* built across the road. At the same time men appeared on all the hilltops and ridges, and stones were rolled down the shoots. Seeing that the enemy was in great strength and very strongly posted, Ross considered it useless to attempt to force a way through to Reshun and decided to retire on the Koragh. Lieutenant Jones with ten men was sent back to seize the Koragh end of the defile in order to cover the withdrawal of the remainder. But the enemy had already closed this exit. All but two of Jones's small party were wounded; and the attempt to break through was abandoned for the time being. Ross and his men took shelter in some caves on the river bank. Of the sixty riflemen who had started with him from Buni, four had been killed and fourteen wounded, two followers were also casualties.

An effort was made to break through to Koragh after dark. But the enemy was on the alert, and the attempt was foiled by a regular avalanche of rocks and large stones propelled down a wide shoot that ran right down into the river across the track. A return was made to the caves.

Later in the night an attempt was made to scale a very steep spur near the caves so as to gain the crest of the ridge above. A prolonged effort to reach the top, during which one man fell and was killed, failed when a precipice was encountered and no way of getting round it could be found. Again Ross returned to the caves. It was by this time almost daybreak, and everyone was dead beat.

The detachment remained in the caves throughout the daylight hours of 9 March, and Ross decided that during the night his party must attempt to break through to Koragh at all costs. He started off at 2 a.m. on the 10th, accompanied by all men capable of moving. The enemy, unfortunately, was thoroughly on the alert and kept up a heavy fire, in addition to rolling rocks down the wide shoot which has been referred to previously. Ross was shot dead, and many men became casualties from injuries inflicted by the torrent of rocks and stones. Only Lieutenant Jones, seventeen men and two followers succeeded in forcing their way out to the plain at the Koragh end of the defile.

There a stand was made for a short time in case any more men might get through. Whilst halted, two charges of hostile swordsmen were delivered against Jones's small party. They were repulsed by volley firing, but the enemy then showed signs of moving to intercept Jones's line of retreat. Three more Sikhs had been killed and of the rest Jones, himself, and nine men had been previously wounded. Jones therefore retired slowly on Buni, which was reached at about 6 a.m. The survivors of the disaster comprised only Lieutenant Jones, fourteen Indian ranks and two followers. Those men still alive who failed to get out of the defile with Jones were eventually starved into surrender to the Chitralis, by whom they were massacred. Lieutenant H. J. Jones was later awarded the D.S.O., all the fourteen combatant ranks received the 3rd Class Indian Order of Merit, and the followers were each granted a bonus of three months' pay.

As for the party under Lieutenant Edwardes, this was invested by the Chitralis at Reshun, where it occupied and defended a group of small houses. There it held out until 15 March, when the two British officers were lured out and treacherously made prisoner, the post at the same garrison overwhelmed.

On arrival back at Buni on 10 March, Lieutenant Jones occupied a house in the village and put it into a state of defence. Including the men left behind at Buni by Ross on the 8th, Jones had under him one Indian officer and forty-seven other ranks. He considered it inadvisable to attempt to return to Mastuj without first communicating with the commander at that place, especially as the enemy was reported to have occupied the strong Nisa Gol position between Buni and Mastuj. Efforts to get a message through, however, failed.

At Mastuj Lieutenant Moberly was unable to obtain information and was entirely in the dark as to what had happened at Chitral, Reshun and the Koragh defile. With him at Mastuj were seventy Kashmir infantry, increased to a total of two hundred and thirty on 13 March by the arrival of reinforcements from the Gilgit direction.

He then decided to march down to Buni to find out what had happened. Unable to obtain any coolies for transport purposes, Moberly set out on the 16th with one hundred and fifty men of the Kashmir Rifles–each man being heavily laden and carrying three days' cooked rations. Buni was reached at 5 p.m. on 17 March.

Moberly had meanwhile received information that a large force of the enemy intended that very night to cut off his retreat at the Nisa Gol position, and further that tribesmen were also collecting on the road between Mastuj and Gilgit. He therefore decided to start back for Mastuj at once taking Jones's party with him. Leaving Buni at 7p.m., Moberly arrived at Mastuj safely next morning after marching all night. It was ascertained later that the enemy reached Buni in force only a few hours after the British party had left, and shortly afterwards occupied the Nisa Gol position.

From 22 March onwards Moberly and the troops under him were besieged in the fort at Mastuj. The defence was skilfully conducted and our casualties were but slight. In the 14th Sikhs detachment only one man was slightly wounded. The enemy made no serious attempt to assault but kept up a constant fire on the fort. During the first week when an assault was expected the men were kept constantly on duty on the fort walls. Snow or sleet fell almost continuously and sentry duty was most harassing. Colonel Kelly with a force form Gilgit raised the siege on 9 April. He set out again four days later for the relief of Chitral, but the remnant of B Company 14th Sikhs was left behind as part of the garrison of Mastuj.

DEFENCE OF CHITRAL.

To return to events at Chitral. The fort there, standing near the river, was badly situated for purposes of defence. It was commanded on three sides at about six hundred yards distance, inside cover was poor; and in the immediate vicinity numerous large trees masked the field of fire from the parapet. The fort, built of rough masonry, was eighty yards square with walls twenty-five feet high and about eight feet thick. At each corner a square tower rose twenty feet above the walls. Water for the fort had to be obtained from the river, and a further tower to guard the route to the water stood fifty yards outside the north face on the edge of the river. There were stables and outhouses between this water tower and the north face. A walled garden extended for one hundred and fifty yards from the east face, and there was a summer-house close to the garden wall forty yards away from the south-eastern tower.

The number of persons within the fort when it became invested on 3 March totalled five hundred and forty-three (including eighty-five followers and fifty-two Chitralis). Captain Townshend at once took steps to organise the defence on a proper basis, to provide better cover for the defenders, and generally to be ready to stand a siege of considerable length. It was estimated that, by issuing half-rations, the supplies would last for two and a half months. There were three hundred rounds of ammunition per man for the Martini-Henry rifles of the Sikhs, and two hundred and eighty rounds per man for the Snider rifles of the Kashmir troops.

The siege began in earnest on 4 March, when the enemy fired all day long into the fort. The Sikh company was at first detailed to man the south face and the keep. On the night of 7 March, however the enemy made a determined effort to set fire to the water tower. The effort was frustrated but it was made evident that the Kashmir sepoys had been so shaken by the action of 3 March that they could not be trusted to defend an important point on the safety of which the lives of the garrison depended. The Sikhs therefore transferred to the north and west faces.

From 8 to 14 March nothing of importance occurred but the garrison was fully engaged in erecting and improving defences and in effecting demolitions outside the fort.

On the night of the 14th the enemy made an attack on the western face, but was repulsed with little difficulty by the steady volleys fired by a section of A Company under Subadar Gurmukh Singh.

The river was low at this season, and there was a space of some thirty yards between the door of the water tower and the water's edge. One of the first measures taken during the siege had therefore been to construct a covered way from the tower to the water. On 15 March the end of the covered way was widened and strengthened and occupied at night by a post of six Sikhs.

On 16 March a letter from Lieutenants Edwards and Fowler was brought under a flag of truce to the British Agent informing him of their capture by the enemy at Resun. A truce was now arranged and lasted for seven days, during which negotiations for the release of the two officers were conducted by Surgeon Major Robertson. These, however, ended fruitlessly on 23 March, when the white flags were hauled down and hostilities were renewed.

The enemy's efforts were now mainly directed against the communication between the fort and its water supply; and strong piquets had to be posted outside the fort to guard the waterway. Twenty men of the 14th were placed in the *sangar* near the water's edge, and these were supported by piquets of Kashmir Rifles in the water tower and the stables in rear. The men in the *sangar* had an unpleasant duty, as there was always about six inches of water in it; nor was there any protection from the heavy rain and snow which fell almost continuously during March. The duty was, however, accepted cheerfully and eagerly by the Sikhs as a post of honour, and their vigilance was most praiseworthy.

On 6 April the enemy occupied the summer-house, situated only forty yards away from the south-eastern tower. At about 5 a.m. on the 7th a heavy fire was opened on the western and northern faces of the fort, and at the same time a half-hearted attack was delivered against the waterway. This was quickly broken up by the steady Sikh volleys. Under cover of these diversions, however, the enemy–unnoticed by the Kashmir sentries–contrived to pile up and set alight a large heap of wood at the base of the south-eastern tower. The fire set light to the projecting ends of the beams of which the tower was in great part built, and it was with the greatest difficulty that the conflagration was extinguished. The fire had caught mainly at the corner of the tower, and the enemy kept up a continuous fusillade at short range on all loopholes and openings in the fort. Six Sikhs were sent to reinforce the garrison of the tower, and it was mainly owing to their exertions and to the excellent behaviour of the Panyali levies and the *bhisties* that the fire was finally got under control after six hours of hard work.

Sepoy Bhola Singh of the 14th was subsequently awarded the 3rd Class Indian Order of Merit for his gallantry on this occasion. After being wounded in one arm whilst helping to put out the fire, he continued to empty water on the blaze with the other arm, although continuously exposed to the enemy.

On 8 April, Subadar Gurmukh Singh submitted a petition from the men of the 14th asking to be allowed to man all the four Fort towers, as well as the water *sangar*, i.e. all the most vitally important points of the British defences. Captain Townshend, recognising that the safety of the garrison depended on the vigilance of the sentries and that only the Sikhs could be trusted to be fully alert, accepted the suggestion. Accordingly, a party of six Sikhs under a non-commissioned officer was henceforward quartered in each tower, whilst the water *sangar* continued to be held by twenty Sikhs with two non-commissioned officers. These parties lived on their posts and continued to do so until the end of the siege.

On 11 April attacks in strength were made against both the east and west faces of the fort, but were repulsed without difficulty. For the next five days the enemy was apparently inactive, but there was much noise and shouting each night in the garden and summer-house. Little attention was paid to this until it occurred to someone that the noise might be intended to drown the sound of the picking of a mine from the summer-house to the south-eastern tower. The sentries were then warned to listen carefully for any such sound. During the night of the 16th one of the sentries in the lower storey of the south-eastern tower reported that he heard the noise of picking. Townshend himself went up and listened, but could hear nothing. In the morning however, it was clearly evident not only that a mine was being made, but that it had reached a point within twelve feet of the fort wall.

Townshend decided upon a sortie that same day to destroy the mine. Lieutenant Harley was detailed for this duty, with forty Sikhs and sixty men of the Kashmir Rifles. His orders were to capture the summer-house and destroy the mine.

The sortie party assembled at the gate of the east face at 4 p.m. on 17 April, the Sikhs in front. Two bags of powder were carried. The gate was opened and Harley passed out, closely followed by his men. Momentary shelter was taken behind a small platform opposite the gate till about a dozen men were collected, when Harley charged with these straight at the summer-house, the others following as they emerged from the fort. About eighty yards of open ground had to be crossed. The summer-house was occupied by a number of Pathans covering the men working in the mine. They fired a volley into the assaulting party as it closed with them killing a man on either side of Harley and wounding another. They then fled down the garden wall, stopped at the far end, threw up a barricade of fascines with great rapidity and, from this cover, opened a galling fire at about one hundred yards range. Harley told off a certain number of his men to keep them in check and then sought for the mine shaft.

This lay outside the summer-house behind the garden wall. It was concealed with fascines, and was not found for some time. Harley with six Sikh volunteers then jumped down the mine shaft. At once, about twenty Chitralis armed with swords tried to dash out; but they were all bayoneted as they came out of the mine entrance. Harley then proceeded to lay the powder bags in position previous to tamping; but it was found that the powder hose, prepared as a substitute for a fuse, had become broken in the scuffle, and only about ten feet of it was left. While preparing to fix this, two or three of the enemy's working party who had remained in the mine came rushing out. The sepoys standing at the mouth of the mine fired on them, whereupon the powder immediately exploded. Harley was knocked down and the clothes of several sepoys were burnt; but, fortunately, the force of the explosion expended itself up the length of the mine, laying it open from end to end and killing six Chitralis who had remained in it.

Harley's task was now completed, and he and his party rushed back to the fort. A proof of the cool and steady way in which the work was done is found in the fact that not only were all arms and accoutrements of the dead and wounded taken back to the fort, but also a number of the enemy's rifles and swords. The casualties incurred in the sortie totalled twenty-one, the Sikhs having three killed and five wounded. The enemy's loss was estimated at one hundred.

The siege was now nearly over. On the night of 18 April a man came to the fort and reported that the enemy had fled and that British troops were close at hand. His news proved to be true. On the 20th, Colonel Kelly arrived with his relief force from Gilgit, and information was received of the near approach of Sir Robert Low's army of fifteen thousand men from the south.

The casualties of A Company, 14th Sikhs, during the defence of Chitral were five men killed and eleven wounded, while one *bhisti* was killed and another wounded. These figures are not excessive, but unquestionably the behaviour of the company was very fine throughout the siege. Extremely well commanded, the Sikhs, as Captain Townshend wrote in his report:

> …never murmured, took everything calmly–the overwork, the half-ration of *atta*, the over fatigues, practically getting no rest: they slept in accoutrements and on their alarm posts throughout the siege. The spirit of the 14th Sikhs was our admiration; the longer the siege lasted the more eager they became to teach the enemy a lesson. There could not be finer soldiers than these men of the 14th Sikhs, and they were our sheet anchor in the siege.

And in his *Relief of Chitral* Younghusband wrote: 'It was the discipline ingrained in these men that saved the garrison. As long as a Sikh was on sentry, while Sikhs were holding a threatened point, Captain Townsend had nothing to fear.'[7]

---

[7]Major General Sir George John Younghusband and Lieutenant Colonel Sir Francis Edward Younghusband, *The Relief of Chitral* (London: Macmillan & Co., 1895).

All ranks of the garrison were awarded a bonus of six months' pay, and the following rewards were granted to officers and men of the 14th Sikhs for their services during the siege:

Lieutenant H. K. Harley D.S.O., promotion to rank of captain antedated three years, and to be promoted brevet major on attaining the rank of captain.

Subadar Gurmukh Singh – Second Class of the Order of British India, with the title of Bahadur.

Jemadar Atar Singh and seven other ranks – Third Class of the Indian Order of Merit.

Although only one company of the Regiment was concerned in the siege, the 14th Sikhs were granted the honour of inscribing 'DEFENCE OF CHITRAL' on their Colours.

In May 1895 the sick and wounded of A and B Companies were evacuated from Chitral and Mastuj to Gilgit. They were detained there for about three months and finally rejoined battalion headquarters at Ferozepore in September. The remainder of the two companies marched under Lieutenant Harley from Chitral on 1 June and, proceeding via Dir and the Malak, reached Ferozepore on the 25th of that month.

On 25 August 1895, Lieutenant Colonel J. W. Hogge C.I.E. was appointed commandant *vice* Colonel W.V. Ellis.

It was in 1895 that a step – more nominal than real – towards the unification of the Indian Army was taken by the abolition of the Presidency armies. The Army of India now became divided into four commands, Madras, Bombay, Bengal and Punjab. In actual fact the change localised the Indian units for peace service even more than hitherto. Regiments retained the numbers and designations that they held in the old Presidency armies. Thus the 14th Sikhs, although allotted to the Punjab Command, retained their official title of 14th (Ferozepore Sikh) Regiment of Bengal Infantry.

CHAPTER 4
1896–1914

THE TOCHI AND CHINA

Although the 14th Sikhs, after being split up in detachments over a long period, were only concentrated at Ferozepore a few days before the end of 1896, such was the reputation they had gained that in June 1897 they were one of the first battalions to be selected for active service. In the event this turned out to be a misfortune; for the Regiment was employed in a theatre of operations where no actual fighting occurred, and missed participation in the Frontier expeditions farther north in which so many troops were engaged during the winter of 1897–1898.

The first spark in the conflagration that was to blaze all along the North-West Frontier later in the year appeared in the Tochi valley on 10 June 1897, when a sudden and totally unexpected tribal attack was made at Maizar on the escort to the Political Officer in the Tochi. The Government of India issued instructions without delay for the formation of the Tochi Field Force, and on 12 June the 14th Sikhs received orders to mobilise and proceed to Bannu to join the 2nd Brigade.

The 14th were not at the time one of those battalions to which mobilisation equipment had been issued, so that its selection for service was quite unexpected. It was the middle of the hot weather season, and a large number of all ranks were absent on leave. Captain Jones was in temporary command.

TOCHI FIELD FORCE, 1897

The Battalion left Ferozepore by train on 17 June. It travelled by rail to Khushalgarh, and thence marched to Bannu, which was reached on the 25th. The heat being excessive, the marches were all made by night. Colonel Hogge rejoined on 12 July from leave out of India and took over command.

The Tochi Field Force remained in being until January 1808. Of actual fighting there was none; but there was a considerable amount of movement; convoy and other duties were always severe, and the sickness in the force was at all times great. The other units of the 2nd Brigade–3rd Battalion, Rifle Brigade, 6th Jats and 25th Punjabis – were all sent back to India on this account. The 14th Sikhs, however, continued throughout to be the healthiest unit in the Tochi.

On the break-up of the Field Force, Colonel Hogge received the following letter from Brigadier General Brooke, then commanding the 2nd Brigade:

> I cannot speak too highly of the conduct and discipline of your Regiment since I have commanded the brigade. The work and severe duty which has been done under most trying conditions in the Tochi valley during the past summer by your Regiment, and its present serviceable condition, have proved a state of efficiency, endurance and devotion to duty which must be most gratifying to you as their commanding officer, and the services of the 14th Sikhs in this expedition may be ranked as not the least among their previous distinguished records!

Owing to the exceptional healthiness of the Regiment, it was detained after the demobilisation of the Field Force to garrison temporarily the lower posts in the Tochi valley. It was relieved at the end of March 1898, and then marched away, via the Kohat Pass, to its new station, Nowshera.

DETACHMENT IN EAST AFRICA, 1897–1899

In June 1897 a party consisting of one Indian officer (Jemadar Bhagwan Singh, 14th Sikhs) and thirty other ranks, drawn equally from the 14th and 15th Sikhs, the whole under Lieutenant N. A. Macdonald, 14th Sikhs, had left India for service with an expedition under the command of Lieutenant Colonel Macdonald, R.E., in British East Africa. The party rejoined their regiments in May 1899. Of the detachment drawn from the 14th Sikhs, Lieutenant Macdonald and one sepoy were killed and Jemadar Bhagwan Singh and three sepoys wounded during the numerous engagements fought against the Sudanese mutineers and others. Jemadar Bhagwan Singh and three sepoys were awarded the Third Class Indian Order of Merit for continuous and conspicuous gallantry in action, and the Jemadar was subsequently advanced Second Class of the Order. Colonel Macdonald, writing of the party stated: 'This detachment fully maintained the great reputation of the 14th Sikhs and fought with such gallantry that they secured the admiration of all.'

The Regiment remained at Nowshera until July 1900. In April of that year an important change in the organisation of Indian infantry battalions was introduced. Instead of being divided into two wings, each of four companies and each commanded by a British officer, the battalion was now divided into four double-companies each under a British double-company commander. At the same time the establishment of British officers was increased to a total of twelve, viz. commandant, four double-company commanders, six double-company officers and one medical officer. The companies remained, as before, commanded by a subadar with a jemadar as his assistant.

CHINA, 1900–1902

In the summer of 1900 troops were despatched from India to China to join the international forces engaged in relieving the legations besieged at Peking and suppressing the Boxer rebellion. The 14th Sikhs at Nowshera had been employed in rebuilding their lines for the best part of two years, and during this time military training had necessarily been reduced to a minimum. It therefore came as a surprise when, on 25 June, orders were received to mobilise for active service in China. It was learnt later that the Battalion was selected at the special request of General Gaselee, commander of the China Expeditionary Force.

The 14th, under Colonel Hogge, left Nowshera by train for Bombay on 7 July.[8] However owing to some hitch in the arrangements for sea transport, the battalion was ordered to detrain at Khandwa, on 12 July and there await further orders. This was unfortunate, for cholera happened to be prevalent in the Khandwa district. Not till the evening of 23 July did the Regiment once more entrain for Bombay: only to be stopped again a short way farther on, for during the night Lieutenant H. Currie was attacked by cholera. The Regiment detrained at Deolali and went into cholera camp nearby. Lieutenant Currie died in hospital the same day, 24 July. The 14th remained segregated for eighteen days. There was no further case of cholera and the men kept very healthy, but it was a monotonous experience. Heavy monsoon rain fell all day and every day.

The Regiment finally left Deolali on 11 August and, on arrival at Bombay next morning, embarked in the S.S. *Formosa*. She sailed at once into the teeth of the monsoon. The *Formosa* was a small ship; she had been prepared very hurriedly to carry troops, and she was filled to her utmost capacity. For the first five days of the voyage enormous seas were encountered, and everyone on board, good sailor or otherwise, had a miserable time. Half the officers' chargers died of injuries. So bad was the weather that the ship could

---

[8] Thirteen British officers, including the Medical Officer, accompanied the battalion. To make up this total, four British officers from the 15th and 45th Sikhs were attached to the 14th.

not put in to Colombo as intended, but had to pass round to the south of Ceylon.

After touching at Singapore and Hong-Kong, the *Formosa* reached Shanghai on 5 September. The 14th disembarked and went into camp on a site adjoining the river bank in the Hongkew area, about a mile from the centre of the International Settlement. Long before this date the besieged legations at Peking had been relieved, and to all intents and purposes there was no more fighting. The 2nd Brigade of the China Expeditionary Force was detailed to garrison Shanghai. In addition to the 14th Sikhs, the Brigade (under Major General O'Moore Creagh) included the 2nd Rajputs, 30th Baluchis and 1/4th Gurkhas.

The 2nd Brigade remained intact at Shanghai till April 1901. Conditions were entirely peaceful. The winter climate, though cold and damp in camp, was good on the whole. For the British officers the seven months spent at Shanghai were a most pleasant period. There were many amenities unobtainable in the ordinary Indian cantonment. Facilities for sport and games were excellent. Many of the younger officers much enjoyed the Rugby football. Hospitality abounded. There was much entertaining, and great fraternisation with the many naval officers who were in warships actually at Shanghai, or made constant visits thither from the British fleet lying off Woosung.

By the spring of 1901 the total of foreign troops of many nationalities in North China was considerable. It was decided to reduce the size of the British contingent, and General Gaselee with much of his force returned to India. General Creagh stayed on as commander of the British forces remaining in North China, with his headquarters at Tientsin. The 2nd Brigade was broken up as a formation, and the 14th Sikhs and 4th Gurkhas were transferred farther north.

The 14th left Shanghai in three groups. The first portion including battalion headquarters sailed on 20 April, the second at the beginning of May and the third at the end of that month. The headquarter portion arrived at Taku on 24 April and proceeded at once by rail to Yangtsun, between Tientsin and Peking.

There existed at this time only two railways in China. One ran from Tongku (Taku) via Tientsin to Peking; the other extended northwards from Tongku towards Manchuria. Most of the foreign powers had military detachments at Peking and Tientsin. The management of the railways was solely in British hands, and the local security of the railway stations and permanent way was a British responsibility. There was a small British garrison at every railway station. For the security of the country, some miles on either side of the railway line, various nations were made individually responsible for different areas.

At Yangtsun the headquarters of the 14th Sikhs were comfortably housed in buildings adjoining the railway station. Two detachments were sent out at once to other posts and several more when the remainder of the Battalion arrived.

In the middle of May battalion headquarters were moved to the Imperial Hunting Lodge, three miles distant from Huangtsun railway station and ten miles from Peking. The Hunting Lodge was a delightful spot. There was ample accommodation in large airy buildings set in the midst of an oriental garden surrounded by undulating park-like country. Fifty Chinese ponies were handed over to the Regiment and a mounted infantry section was formed. This was employed in patrolling the railway line and in occasional expeditions after bandits, the only approach to fighting experienced by the 14th in China.

Headquarters remained at the Hunting Lodge till the middle of September and then moved to Yangtsun again for two months. At the end of November they were transferred to Tongku, where they remained until the Battalion sailed for India. The Regiment continued to be split up in many detachments. In December 1901 the distribution was:

Tongku	Headquarters and 1½ companies
Peking	1½ companies
Tientsin	1½ companies
Garrisons of ten railway stations between Tongku and Peking	3½ companies

In October 1901, Colonel Hogge departed on leave to England pending retirement, and Lieutenant Colonel A. E. Pelhamn Burn (33rd Punjabis) was appointed temporary commandant.

The winter in North China is extremely cold, the thermometer often descending below zero, but, except for occasional gales and blizzards, the winter of 1901–1902 was generally dry and still, with an invigorating crispness in the air; nearly every day was sunny. All ranks of the British forces were liberally supplied with warm clothing and lived quite comfortably.

The 14th Sikhs finally left China on 29 July from Taku on the R.I.M.S. *Clive*.

The two years spent in North China were a most interesting experience. Especially interesting, and of no small educational value, was the contact with troops of so many other nations; Russians, Japanese, Americans, French, Germans, Italians. In the circumstances there was very little friction. The British officers got on extremely well with the Americans and Japanese; the latter were effusively friendly. Russian and Italian officers, also, seemed to find much in common with us. The French and Germans were perhaps less friendly than the rest, but there were exceptions. The compiler of this narrative, for instance, spent four winter months at the little station of Langfang, the only British officer there. He was an almost daily guest at the Officers' Mess of a German battalion quartered nearby, and although a very junior subaltern, was always welcomed, with the utmost cordiality.

During the sojourn of the Regiment in China, its official title underwent another modification. In 1901 it became the 14th (Ferozepore) Sikh Infantry, and the connection with Bengal was finally severed.

MULTAN,1902–1905

The 14th Sikhs disembarked at Calcutta on 25 August 1902 and thence went by train to Multan. There they were stationed until February 1905.

Lieutenant Colonel W. E. Bunbury, transferred from the 28th Punjabis, was appointed commandant in August 1902 and joined the Regiment at Multan. In January 1903 the Rajah of Nacho (His Highness Sir Hire Singh Malwandar Bahadur, G.C.S.I. G.C.I.E.) was appointed honorary Colonel of the 14th Sikhs and held this distinction until his death. In the same year the Regiment was re-armed with the long .303 Lee-Metford rifle. Its title also was once more modified, to become the 14th Ferozepore Sikhs.

The period at Multan coincided with the advent of Lord Kitchener as Commander-in-Chief and the introduction of more intensive training in the Army in India. It is unnecessary to dwell upon the details of training. Tactics and methods of training are constantly changing; high morale, good discipline, the smartness that is so great an aid to discipline, and esprit de corps will always be essentials for a good regiment. That these essentials were not lost sight of during the next few years is evident from the description applied to the 14th Sikhs by the Commander of the Lahore Division in his annual report for the year 1906,'A splendid battalion, full of esprit de corps and priding itself on its steady drill and discipline.'

Incidentally, the South African War of 1899–1902 had exercised for a short time a baleful influence on British Army training. Smartness was often at a discount; skilful scouting and skirmishing appeared to be the only ideals; the best soldier, apparently was he who was most proficient in the art of taking cover! Fortunately, saner counsels soon prevailed.

The year 1903 saw the abolition of that misleading designation Indian Staff Corps, and henceforward the British officers as well as the Indian ranks belonged to one corps, the Indian Army. In the same year units of the Indian Army were renumbered and in many cases given new designations. All mention of the designations of the old Presidency armies was omitted. The localisation of units in certain areas for peace service was abolished – in theory at any rate.

In 1904 the so-called Kitchener Test was introduced, in order to stimulate efficiency in training by bringing in the element of competition. On a fixed syllabus of subjects, regiments were tested by a committee of senior officers and allotted marks, as in an ordinary school examination. The 14th Sikhs did a wonderful performance in a forced march test carried out from a brigade training camp at Muzaffargarh near Multan early in 1905. Equipped in full field service order, the Battalion covered fifteen miles along a dusty road in three hours and forty minutes. Not one man fell out, and each double-company at the end of the course was marching in perfect order, well closed up, with the lines of fours correctly dressed. The Battalion was under the temporary command of Major H. J. Jones, D.S.O.

It was at Multan, after their return from China, that the game of hockey was first taken up seriously by the 14th Sikhs. Prior to this there had been no organised games in which the rank and file participated. For many years previously there had been periodical athletic sports meetings, quoit-throwing competitions and so on: but these were only occasional affairs. At hockey the men soon became proficient and were always very keen.

FEROZEPORE, 1905–1907

The Regiment moved to Ferozepore in March 1905 and remained there for two and a half years. Training was carried out as intensively as it had been at Multan, and the 14th were in a high state of efficiency. In November 1905 the Battalion marched to Rawalpindi and took part in the manoeuvres culminating in the big review before the Prince of Wales on 8 December.

On 1 January 1906 the Regiment was honoured by the appointment of H.R.H. the Prince of Wales as Colonel-in-Chief, and its title was altered to 14th Prince of Wales Own Ferozepore Sikhs. Lieutenant Colonel W. E. Bunbury, Lieutenant and Adjutant F. E. G. Talbot and Subadar Major Bhagwan Singh were presented to the Prince of Wales at Benares in February, and the Subadar Major was later decorated with the Medal of the Royal Victorian Order.

During the year the Battalion was re-armed with the short magazine Lee-Enfield rifle.

THE SAMANA, 1907–1908

The 14th Sikhs moved in November 1907 by route march from Ferozepore to Hangu and Fort Lockhart. The impressions of Sir Henry Craik, a touring Member of Parliament, who happened to see the Battalion on the march near Lahore, were thus recorded in an article in *The Scotsman*:

> The other day during our morning ride we passed a regiment, the 14th Sikhs, in marching order on their way from Ferozepore through Lahore to the frontier, and a finer lot of men it has never been my lot to see. Their uniform was admirably serviceable and at the same time strikingly picturesque; long blue tunics, loosely made;[9] khaki coloured trousers white pugarees,[10] each with the war-quoit twisted in its folds. Without exception they were much above middle height and their sergeants as elders of the corps, were models of dignity with their long grey beards.[11] They kept perfect rank and stepped out in perfect time, but at the same time with an easy long swing that it would be hard for any European regiment to rival.

On arrival at Hangu the headquarters and half the Battalion remained in camp there, whilst the remaining half garrisoned Fort Lockhart. This distribution continued throughout the winter. but in the summer of 1908 the whole Battalion was concentrated at Fort Lockhart.

---

[9] The men happened to be wearing their blue-grey greatcoat-capes over their khaki blouses.
[10] The pugarees were khaki coloured. Perhaps they appeared to be white when covered with the thick dust from the road.
[11] The dust no doubt was again responsible for the 'greyness' of the beards which, incidentally, were not long.

In March 1908 the 14th Sikhs for the first time were the winners of the Punjab Native Army Hockey Tournament held at Lahore. In the previous year they had been defeated in the final by the 15th Sikhs by an odd goal: this time the two battalions met once again in the final, and the result was exactly reversed.

Colonel Bunbury vacated command in August 1908 and was succeeded by Lieutenant Colonel H. J. Jones.

QUETTA, 1908–1910

In October of that year the Regiment marched in relief from Fort Lockhart to Quetta – a long and interesting march along the edge of the frontier via Kohat Valley, Bannu, Tank, the Gomal valley the Zhob valley, Fort Sandeman and Hindubagh. The 14th remained at Quetta for two years. Throughout the whole of 1910 half the Battalion was detached to garrison Robat, a remote and isolated spot near the point of junction of Afghanistan, Persia and British Baluchistan. The ostensible object was to prevent gun-runners from the Persian Gulf passing through British territory on their way to Afghanistan, though there was nothing to stop them from gaining Afghanistan by passing through Persian territory a few miles away. Possibly, however, there were also other reasons, of a strategic nature, for troops were kept at Robat till after the outbreak of the Great War.

After his accession to the Throne in 1910, H.M. King George V continued to be Colonel-in-Chief of the Regiment, whose designation then became the 14th King George's Own Ferozepore Sikhs. At the same time the Regiment was permitted to retain the Plume of the Prince of Wales as one of its badges in addition to the Royal and Imperial Cypher.

LORALALI, 1910–1913

In October 1910 the 14th moved from Ouetta to Loralai, where it remained until early in 1913.

In May 1911, Subadar Major Bhagwan Singh and Jemadar Jaimal Singh went to England with other selected representatives of the Indian Army to attend the Coronation of King George V.

Being stationed so far away, the 14th Sikhs did not as a regiment form part of the troops assembled at Delhi in December 1911 for the Coronation Durbar; but a representative detachment was sent there. This consisted of Colonel Jones, Captain Talbot, two Indian officers and eighteen other ranks. Captain Talbot did duty during the Durbar as extra aide-de-camp to the King. Whilst at Delhi, His Majesty presented engravings of himself and the Queen to the Officers' Mess, and Subadar Gulab Singh was decorated with the Medal of the Royal Victorian Order.

Colonel Jones's tenure of command expired in August 1912, when he was succeeded by Lieutenant Colonel P. C. Palin.

PESHAWAR, 1913–1914

The 14th moved from Loralai in February 1913 to be stationed at Peshawar, marching direct from Loralai to Ghazi Ghat and thence travelling by train. Soon after arrival at Peshawar, Subadar Major Bhagwan Singh was selected as one of the four Indian Orderlies to the King for that year and spent the early summer months in England.

All ranks of the Regiment were particularly happy and contented at Peshawar in 1913–1914, and never has the reputation of the corps stood higher. Training reached a very high standard – morale and discipline were as nearly perfect as is humanly possible. Colonel Palin was a splendid commanding officer. The British officers were an exceedingly happy family, many of whom were to lose their lives in 1915. Incidentally, their athletic achievements were outstanding. In Peshawar they won the tennis and golf competitions, and an officers' team of the 14th beat every other unit, British and Indian, at hockey and cricket. The Indian Army cricket eleven of the Peshawar District, which beat the Rifle Brigade in the final match for the Jamasjee Cup, included no less than nine officers of the 14th Sikhs.

There have been such drastic changes in the organisation and conditions of service of Indian infantry in recent years that perhaps it may not be out of place to recall briefly the situation as it was just before the outbreak of the Great War. The bulk of the infantry, including the 14th Sikhs, were organised as single battalion regiments; and each regiment was very much a self contained and independent unit, in spite of the grouping of linked battalions. Much of the administration and interior economy was still based on that system of the old irregular corps which was introduced generally into the Army after the Mutiny of 1857. The regiment trained its own recruits and to some extent also enrolled them. Except on active service, the men paid for their rations, which were provided by regimental arrangement under the control of the commanding officer. In great degree the regiment clothed itself. The interior economy and internal organisation of an Indian battalion was a complicated business. Though in theory the system was the same for all battalions, in practice there was much variation. The internal administration of the 14th Sikhs was excellent, and this had been the case for many years past; nevertheless, the system in general was ill adapted to the conditions of war on a big scale.

Like the majority of Indian battalions, the 14th Sikhs had a peace establishment of 15 British officers (including a medical officer), 16 Indian officers and 806 Indian other ranks. There were also a number of followers or non-combatants, both public and private. The war establishment comprised 13 British officers (including the medical officer), 17 Indian officers and 736 Indian other ranks, together with 85 followers. The battalion organised into headquarters, four double-companies and a machinegun section of two Maxim guns. A double-company was commanded by a British officer, with another as his assistant; each company, comprising two Indian officers and 87 or 88 Indian other ranks, was divided into four sections. The large company and platoon organisation had not yet been introduced into the Indian Army.

On mobilisation, the battalion had to form its own depot at its regimental centre –Multan in the case of the 14th Sikhs. To the depot were sent one or two British officers, administrative and clerical staff, untrained recruits and the necessary instructors, men medically unfit, and others – if any – surplus to war establishment. In spite of the higher peace establishment, however, and in spite of the existence of a reserve liable to recall to the Colours on mobilisation, it was rare for a battalion to take the field at full strength without having men from other units drafted into it. This was mainly due to the unsatisfactory reserve system.

CHAPTER 5
1914–1915

THE GREAT WAR:
EGYPT AND GALLIPOLI, UP TO 27 JUNE 1915

When war with Germany broke out in August 1914 there seemed little chance of the 14th Sikhs being sent on service overseas, for it was thought that the situation on the North-West Frontier would not permit of any units being withdrawn from Peshawar. It was therefore a surprise when mobilisation orders were received on the evening of 12 October.

Mobilisation was completed on the 27th, and the Battalion completed to war establishment plus ten percent. First reinforcement by the inclusion of one hundred reservists and thirty men drafted from the 45th Sikhs left Peshawar by train for Karachi on 28 October amid scenes of great enthusiasm. A distribution list of the British officers of the 14th Sikhs on 29 October, 1914, is given in Appendix II (page 162). Captain Field, a former officer of the Regiment, who had rejoined for war service from the Political Department, was left in charge of the depot at Multan.

On arrival at Karachi the 14th embarked in the transport *City of Manchester*, which sailed on 3 November in company with nine other vessels under the escort of H.M.S. *Duke of Edinburgh*. The whole of the 20th Indian Infantry Brigade, under Brigadier General H. V. Cox, 14th Sikhs, 69th Punjabis, 89th Punjabis and 1/6th Gurkhas, were accommodated in vessels of this convoy. Its destination was Egypt.

SHAIKH SAID, 10–11 November 1914

On the way to Egypt occurred the affair of Shaikh Said. This was a minor operation in which the 14th Sikhs did not come under fire; it may therefore be summarised very briefly.

Shaikh Said lies on the Arabian coast opposite the British island of Perim. The Turks had a small post there, and General Cox was instructed to land a force to destroy the Turkish defence works and armament. This task was carried out successfully in the face of only slight opposition. Under cover of gunfire from H.M.S. *Duke of Edinburgh*, the 69th and 89th Punjabis were landed in boats on the morning of 10 November and then advanced and drove back the enemy. The 14th Sikhs formed the reserve. They did not begin to leave their ship until 2p.m. To transport the men ashore there were only six boats available, and these were taken to the beach by naval pinnaces in tows of three each. Progress was slow, and the Battalion did not complete its disembarkation till nearly daybreak on 11 November. It then moved forward and covered the 23rd Sikh Pioneers whilst the latter were engaged on demolition work, the two Punjabi battalions meanwhile being re-embarked in their transports. The whole force put ashore was back on board ship by 5:30 p.m. British casualties totalled seventeen. The flag which was flying over the Turkish post was discovered among the ruined defences by a sepoy of the 14th and is now amongst the trophies in the Officers' Mess.[12]

---

[12] The sepoy who discovered it attached no sentimental value to the flag. He had spotted the flagstaff as good material for firewood, had taken of the flag and thrown it away and was much disappointed at not being allowed to take the staff back to the ship; for the Sikhs had experienced difficulty in cooking with coke in the ship's galleys.

Continuing the voyage up the Red Sea, the convoy of British vessels reached Suez on 16 November: but the 14th Sikhs did not disembark until the 21st. They moved by rail the same day to Port Said. The Battalion was now a unit of the British forces defending the Suez Canal.

DEFENCE OF SUEZ CANAL, 1914–1915

The defences of the Canal were organised in sectors; the 29th Brigade being allotted to the northern sector, of which General Cox became the commander. At this stage of the war the defence works were mostly on the west bank of the canal. Some important posts, however, such as Qantara, were on the east bank; their object being to act partly as bridgeheads to the various ferries across the canal and partly as points to launch counter-attacks. In the northerly sector General Cox established his headquarters at Qantara. His troops – a large brigade group – were distributed in a number of posts, but the bulk of them were concentrated at Qantara. The 14th Sikhs arrived there on 2 December from Port Said.

Qantara consisted merely of the railway station on the west bank of the canal and the quarantine station on the east bank. For several weeks the troops were kept busy working on the extension and improvement of the defences on the east bank. There were two entrenched camps; these were covered by an outpost position, about one mile east of the camps, held at night by a line of piquets. By day outpost troops occupied a position of observation on a hill some four miles to the north-east of Qantara on the route to Qatia. The day position was held by two double-companies, provided by battalions in turn; the night piquets were permanently allotted to units. Reconnaissances were carried out daily by the cavalry and camelry of General Cox's command, but, for the infantry, life was at first rather monotonous. There was no sign of the enemy until the end of January 1915.

Contact with the Turks first occurred on 25 January, when Cox's mounted troops came in touch with a small hostile force which had reached a hill two miles east of our daylight observation post. At dusk our advanced troops withdrew as usual from this post. Next morning a column marched out from Qantara under Lieutenant Colonel Bruce (1/6th Gurkhas), who had instructions to reconnoitre and then to drive away the enemy if his strength and position were not too strong. The infantry of the column comprised half the 6th Gurkhas and two double-companies of the 14th Sikhs. After making a reconnaissance, Colonel Bruce decided to attack; but fresh instructions from Qantara then reached him, limiting his activities to observation only. In the afternoon he withdrew his force to Qantara. The Turks made no attempt to follow up.

At about 3:45 a.m. on 28 January a body of the enemy, about two hundred strong, attacked the piquet of our outpost line which lay astride the route from Qatia to Qantara. This piquet consisted of half E Company, 14th Sikhs, under Captain Channer.

The Battalion scouts under Lieutenant Meade had given timely notice, and the attack was repulsed without difficulty. Jemadar Partap Singh and one sepoy were killed – the first war casualties in the Battalion. By 4:30 a.m. the Turks were in retreat, and were harassed in their withdrawal by gunfire from H.M.S. *Swiftsure*, which kept a searchlight beam playing on them. They left behind three dead and one wounded. At daybreak a British detachment moved out from Qantara, but was not permitted to go beyond the usual observation post four miles away. There it remained till dusk, when it returned to camp.

The Turks delivered their general attack against the canal defences on 3 February. Qantara was not one of the enemy's principal objectives, but it was attacked by a weak force very early in the morning. The enemy was easily repulsed, and was followed up after daybreak by a column which included two double-companies of the 14th Sikhs. Pursuit, however, was permitted only for a short distance. The total British casualties at Qantara during the day were twenty-two: there were none in the 14th Sikhs.

After 3 February life again became peaceful and rather monotonous, and this state of affairs continued for over two months. From 22 March onwards the Battalion provided garrisons for a number of posts along the canal bank. Only one incident is worth recording.

Early in the morning of 6 April Jemadar Narain Singh, whilst patrolling from a post five miles north of Qantara, discovered tracks leading eastward from the canal. He followed them up and came upon an abandoned packing-case, together with two poles which had apparently been used to carry it. Suspecting that the case had contained a mine, the Jemadar reported the matter to superior authority. This led to the Navy dragging the Canal in the vicinity; with the result that on 11 April an anchored mine was found just outside the buoyed channel.[13]

GALLIPOLI 1915

Instructions to be in readiness to move to another sphere of operations (not specified) were received by the 14th Sikhs on 10 April. By the 20th, 29th Indian Brigade was concentrated at Port Said. Six days later the 14th embarked in the transport *Dunluce Castle*, and on the 27th the convoy of ships carrying the Indian Brigade sailed from Port Said. It arrived off Cape Helles on 30 April, about midday. To most of the Regiment this was the first day on which it was definitely known that they were to join the British force under General Sir Ian Hamilton in Gallipoli.

The spectacle on nearing the Dardanelles was impressive. A large fleet of warships, transports and trawlers lay off the Gallipoli peninsula, and the guns of the warships were continuously in play, bombarding various Turkish forts on either side of the straits or supporting the Allied troops on shore. The *Dunluce Castle* moored about half a mile from the beach. From the deck of the transport movement on shore could be seen and the sound of rifle and machinegun fire was heard, but nothing was known in the Battalion of the state of affairs on the peninsula. It was imagined that our advanced troops were somewhere on the far side of a long, low hill

---

[13] Jemadar Narain Singh received the special thanks of the commander of the Canal Defences. During the War the Jemadar was awarded the Indian Distinguished Service Medal and Military Cross: he completed his Regimental career as Subadar Major.

which could be seen in the distance and was later learnt to be Achi Baba.

The Indian Brigade did not disembark till next day, 1 May. Units were taken ashore in trawlers and landed at V Beach, near Cape Helles. After disembarkation, the brigade went into bivouac on the high ground nearby.

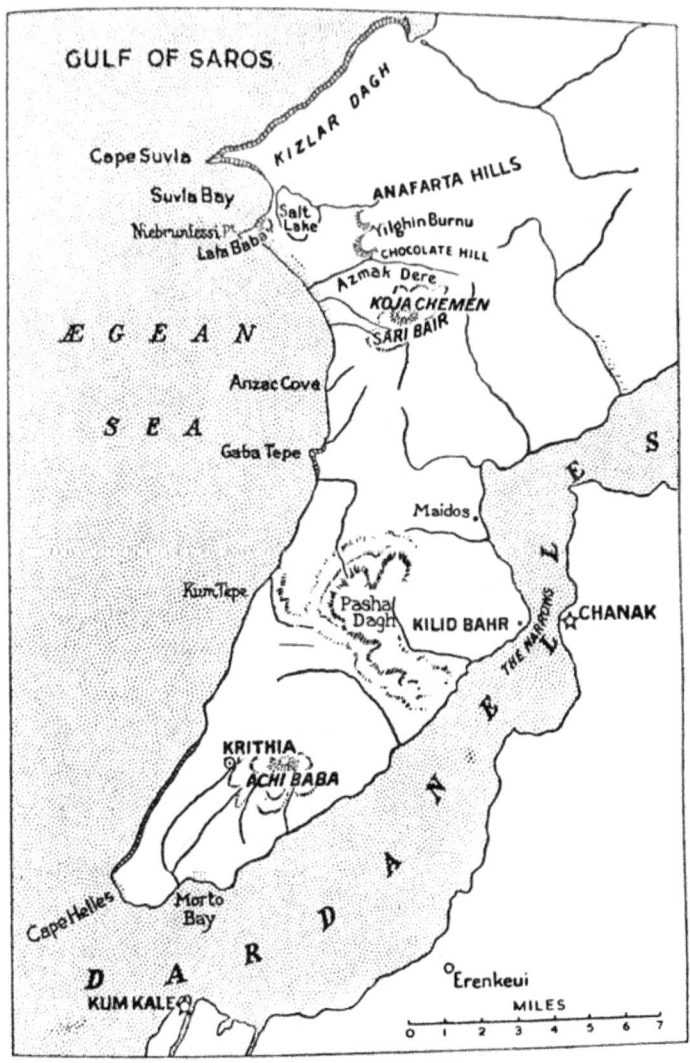

THE GALLIPOLI PENINSULA.
1915.

The distance from the summit of Achi Baba, two hundred feet above the sea, to Cape Helles at the south-western extremity of the Gallipoli peninsula is nearly six miles. On 1 May the Anglo French forces ashore in this area were holding a line, astride the peninsula from sea to sea, three miles in length. This line, barely entrenched, was under three miles distant from Cape Helles, or less than half-way between that point and Achi Baba. The French were on the right and the British on the left. The British 29th Division was in the front line. It had suffered heavy casualties, and the only reserves at hand, in addition to the Indian Brigade were three battalions of the Royal Naval Division

During the evening of 1 May a hostile aeroplane flew over and bombed the Indian Brigade's bivouac, which also received a few shells from guns on the Asiatic side of the Dardanelles. Meanwhile strong working parties from the brigade had been sent to V and W beaches to construct roads and help in the landing of artillery and stores. The state of the beaches was chaotic. Vessels were landing their cargoes as rapidly as they could: but although these were required urgently, there was little storage space and few facilities for sending them forward. No non-military labour was available.

After dark it became cold and later the night was bitter. Officers and men had only khaki drill uniform and their greatcoats. It was too cold to sleep. Not long after 10 p.m. there was a heavy outburst of firing, apparently not far away. Colonel Palin ordered the 14th Sikhs to stand to, and awaited orders. These soon arrived. It was learnt that the Turks had broken through part of the front held by the 29th Division and that the Indian Brigade was to be ready to move at a moment's notice. The situation, however, was restored by local reserves, and the services of the Indian Brigade were not required.

The men stood down and attempted to take what rest they could, despite the cold and a general feeling of tension. About 1 a.m. firing broke out again. This time the weight of the Turkish attack fell upon the left of the French, some of whose Senegalese troops gave way. The situation was critical for a short time, but was restored with British help. The Indian Brigade again stood to arms until the crisis had passed, and the Turkish night attack finally ended without achieving any success. For the men of the Indian Brigade their first night on the peninsula had been a somewhat nerve-racking experience.

On 2 May the Allies attempted to gain ground to their front, and early in the morning the Indian Brigade moved forward to a position from which it could advance to exploit any success. The day's operations, however, produced no fruitful result, and the brigade was not engaged. The 14th Sikhs had two men wounded by Turkish snipers behind our lines. The bravery of these snipers was phenomenal. Left behind by the Turks with a supply of food and ammunition, the men concealed themselves in trees and bushes and inflicted serious losses before being rounded up.

The Indian Brigade bivouacked for the night of 2 May in the fields to which it had moved during the day. There was a considerable amount of intermittent rifle fire, and the ear-splitting noise of Allied artillery firing from close behind gave the impression that a strong Turkish attack was taking place. Actually no hostile infantry attack was pressed. But the atmosphere was tense and the situation must have been considered serious, for Lieutenant Meade and 2nd Lieutenant Savory of the 14th were detailed to reconnoitre the route to the position which would be held in the event of the Indian Brigade having to cover a general withdrawal.

Next morning the brigade returned to its original camp near V Beach. That night the Turks again attacked; this time with determination against the French sector of the Allied front. At 5 a.m. on 4 May the Indian Brigade moved forward to support the French, whose Senegalese troops had been driven from their trenches. Once again, however, the situation was restored by local reserves. The Indian Brigade was not required and by 8:30 a.m. had returned to its camp.

In spite of the exhaustion and heavy casualties of the bulk of the Allied troops at Helles, Sir Ian Hamilton felt it to be essential to gain ground before the enemy had time in which to strengthen his positions and bring up reinforcements. A general advance was therefore ordered for 6 May. The British force at Helles was reorganised; the 125th Brigade (just arrived from Egypt) and the Indian Brigade being attached to the 29th Division, while a temporary composite division was formed of two reinforcing brigades from Anzac and some battalions of the Royal Naval Division.

SECOND BATTLE OF KRITHIA, 6–8 May 1915

At the commencement of the Second Battle of Krithia on 6 May the Indian Brigade was in reserve, about one thousand yards in rear of the British front line. During the day the Allies made almost negligible progress. The Indian Brigade was not seriously engaged. It occupied support trenches and suffered some losses from shellfire, the casualties of the 14th Sikhs being three men killed and thirteen wounded.

Fighting was continued on the 7th. Again no appreciable progress was made. The Indian Brigade remained in reserve and did not move. Casualties in the 14th Sikhs were eight men wounded. Another effort on 8 May once more failed, and the three days' battle ended with the Allied line advanced nowhere more than six hundred yards. The Indian Brigade was not engaged on the 8th. Colonel Palin was slightly wounded in the heel by a spent bullet, but there were no other casualties in the 14th Sikhs that day.

On 9 May the Indian Brigade moved up into front line, relieving the 87th Brigade on the extreme British left. For four days the 14th Sikhs remained in support. Casualties in the Battalion between the 9th and the 12th totalled two men killed and seventeen wounded.

By this time siege warfare may be said to have begun. No further general Allied advance was attempted until 4 June. Until that date efforts were directed upon consolidating and fortifying the front, improving approaches, sapping, reconnaissance and local advances; the last named taking the shape of concentrated attacks on small sections of the enemy's line. Constant fighting continued throughout this period, for the Turks also were by no means inactive.

On the night of 12 May the 1/6th Gurkhas by a skilful and dashing attack gained possession of what became known as Gurkha Bluff, near the sea on the extreme left of the British line. By this feat the Gurkhas advanced their left by about six hundred yards; but their right had not been able to gain ground to the same extent, and by daybreak on the 13th the 1/6th were holding an irregular frontage of about seven hundred yards, with the left half-battalion facing north-east and the right half facing east and extending southward to the Gully Ravine.

During the morning Numbers 1 and 2 Double-Companies of the 14th Sikhs moved up to support the 6th Gurkhas and arrived at about 11 a.m. at the head of a ravine just behind the centre of the left half of the Gurkha line. Meantime, a party of fifty men of Number 4 Double-Company, attempting to work on a communication trench near the western side of Gully Ravine, came under heavy shellfire and was forced to desist with the loss of ten casualties.

At about 4:30 p.m. orders were received for the 14th Sikhs to relieve in front line both the 89th Punjabis and the right half of the 6th Gurkhas. Numbers 3 and 4 Double-Companies were detailed to relieve the Punjabis, and Gurkhas.

During the day, part of the 89th on the right of the Gully Ravine, had gained ground to their front. This forward position was taken over and occupied by Number 4 Double-Company and was entrenched as rapidly as possible directly it became dark. A weak Turkish counterattack was easily repulsed; but unfortunately during most of the night Number 4 Double-Company suffered from the intermittent fire of a battalion in rear which was apparently unaware of our advanced position. Captain Channer (commander of Number 4 Double-Company) was severely wounded.

Meanwhile, on the left, the taking over of the right half of the Gurkha frontage by Numbers 1 and 2 Double-Companies along an irregular line that was only barely entrenched was a somewhat lengthy operation, in the course of which Major Swinley was mortally wounded by a shot in the head. At 7:30 p.m. a company of the Royal Inniskilling Fusiliers, with the battalion machineguns, came up in support and assisted the two double-companies to consolidate their position.

The casualties of the 14th Sikhs in Indian ranks during 13 May were nine killed and twenty-four wounded.

All through the next day the Battalion dug hard to improve its defences. In the evening Lieutenant Spankie was killed by a shot in the head from a Turkish sniper. A fortnight had now passed since the 14th Sikhs landed at Cape Helles. The Battalion had not yet been seriously engaged; indeed, it had only been in the front line for the last two days; nevertheless it had suffered seventy-eight casualties in the Indian ranks and had lost three valuable British officers, two of whom were double-company commanders.

On 15 May two British battalions were posted temporarily to the Indian Brigade in place of the 69th and 89th Punjabis, who left Gallipoli for France. Four British officers from the 89th remained on the peninsula and were attached to the 14th Sikhs. Of these, Captain J. D. Strong took over command of Number 4 and Captain R. S. Engledue that of Number 1 Double-Company (*vice* Major Swinley).

For the next few days the battalion worked steadily on the improvement of its trenches and the communications in rear. Major General Hunter-Weston visited this part of the line on the 17th and congratulated Colonel Palin on the way in which his trenches were kept and on the general appearance of the 14th Sikhs. Although not in large numbers, casualties occurred almost every day. Between 14 and 18 May two men were killed and six wounded.

Now began a period during which our front was advanced by digging a forward line by night, abandoning it by day, and eventually occupying it on the second, or third, night. At first the Turks did not realise what was happening. But on the night of 22 May, when Captain Engledue moved out with B Company to occupy trenches constructed the previous night, he found that a section of trench on his right which had been dug by the 2nd Royal Fusiliers (86th Brigade) was occupied by Turks.

Captain Engledue attacked at once with the bayonet and drove the enemy out. It was then found that a gap existed between B Company's right and the left of the Fusiliers. Before this could be adjusted, the Turks launched a vigorous attack against the Royal Fusiliers and pressed them hard. A Company was immediately ordered up to fill the gap and take the enemy in flank – an operation which was carried out with great dash and was entirely successful. For this prompt action the 14th Sikhs received the thanks of the commander of the Royal Fusiliers. A pleasant sequel followed six years later, when both corps being stationed in the Khyber Pass, the officers of the 2nd Royal Fusiliers presented the officers of the 14th Sikhs with a silver grenade inscribed:

    In Memory of Gallipoli 1915 and the Khyber Pass 1921

Up to the end of May the process of advancing by night and digging in was continued, until the British front line lay at an average distance of under two hundred yards from that of the Turks. Digging parties were disturbed only by intermittent and desultory fire. Lieutenant Meade with the Battalion scouts patrolled nightly up to the enemy's wire, on which he tied pieces of white rag to act as aiming marks in the dark. He never encountered a Turkish patrol.

On 29 May Captain Strong was wounded; sad to say he eventually became completely blind. Lieutenant Fowle took over command of Number 4 Double-Company. Casualties in Indian ranks between 19 and 31 May totalled twenty killed and fourteen wounded. On 1 June the Battalion was strengthened by the arrival from Egypt of its first reinforcement, comprising two British officers and forty-nine Indian ranks.

By this date the Allied force at Helles was organised in two corps: the French Corps and the British VIII Corps under General Hunter-Weston. The British corps consisted of three divisions, the Royal Naval, 42nd and 29th. The last named comprised the 87th, 88th and Indian Brigades, the 86th Brigade having been broken up temporarily. The Allied line had been reorganised in depth in four sectors, the French Corps holding the extreme right and the three

British divisions the other three sectors. The 29th Division was on the left.

The Indian Brigade occupied a frontage of about eight hundred yards on the extreme left of the British line. The 14th Sikhs trench line lay astride the Gully Ravine, the right of the Battalion being in touch with the left of the 4th Worcestershire of the 88th Brigade. The 1st Lancashire Fusiliers, in the centre of the Indian Brigade, held a line across Gully Spur: and the 6th Gurkhas prolonged the left to the cliffs bordering the Aegean Sea. The 1st Royal Inniskilling Fusiliers, stationed in rear, formed the brigade reserve.

THIRD BATTLE OF KRITHIA, 4 June 1915

Sir Ian Hamilton had decided to fight a general action on 4 June with the object of gaining ground along the whole length of the Allied front at Helles. Owing to the trench warfare conditions, only limited objectives of a few hundred yards were allotted to the troops. The plan of attack was worked out in great detail. On 2 and 3 June extensive and thorough preparations were made by the whole force, and full instructions were issued regarding the role to be played by each unit.

On the front of the Indian Brigade, open ground on Gully Spur sloped up north-eastwards towards two lines of Turkish trenches, known as J.10 and J.11, which confronted the Lancashire Fusiliers at distances of two hundred and five hundred yards. The 14th Sikhs, to the right of and below the Fusiliers, were entrenched across Gully Ravine and for one hundred yards on the farther, or eastern side. The ravine was about seventy-five yards wide and forty to fifty deep, the lower portion being covered with low scrub.

Its left edge, where the side of Gully Spur dipped down steeply, was higher than the right edge, from which the ground sloped gradually upward and eastward to a crest line about two hundred yards away. The enemy was known to have several small trenches in the Gully Ravine, and there was also the possibility of machineguns being hidden in positions on the sides commanding the approaches up the gully. Further, fire from the trenches J.10

and J.11 on Gully Spur could sweep not only the bottom of the ravine but also the glacis-like eastern slope and the ground beyond as far as the crest line.

The first objective of the Indian Brigade's attack was the Turkish trench line J.11, the ultimate objective a trench farther on known as J.13. A first wave, or line of attack, was to reach and capture J.11 and establish itself there. A second wave, starting its advance fifteen minutes later than the first, was to push straight through to capture J.13.

Allotted to the first wave were half the 6th Gurkhas, the whole battalion of Lancashire Fusiliers and half the 14th Sikhs. The Fusiliers, in the centre, were to capture J.11 after first clearing the enemy out of J.10. They would be assisted by the Gurkhas on their left and by one double-company of the 14th Sikhs on their right. The duty of the other Sikh double-company in the first wave was to form a connecting link between the right of the Indian Brigade and the left of the 88th Brigade. The second wave was to consist of half each of the 6th Gurkhas, Royal Inniskilling Fusiliers, and 14th Sikhs. Half the Inniskillings were to form brigade reserve.

It was arranged that on 4 June artillery bombardment would be carried out from 8 a.m. to 11:20 a.m. all along the Allied front. The guns would then cease firing for ten minutes during which our infantry would cheer and show fixed bayonets above their trenches to induce the enemy to man his parapets, From 11:30 to 12 noon our guns would bombard the enemy's front line heavily. At 12 o'clock the batteries would increase their range and the first infantry wave would rush out of their trenches to the assault, followed at 12:15 by the second wave.

In the 14th Sikhs Colonel Palin detailed Numbers 2 and 4 Double-Companies for the first wave. Number 2, on the left working up the Gully Ravine and along its western bank was first to assist the Lancashire Fusiliers by taking the trench J.10 in flank, and then to go on with the Fusiliers to the assault of J.11. Number 4 Double-Company, on the right, was to conform to the advance of the 88th Brigade on its right and ensure that no gaps occurred between the 88th and Indian Brigades. Numbers 1 and 3 Double-Companies were allotted to the second wave, Number 1 on the right and Number 3 in the Gully Ravine. The Battalion's two machineguns were not to move forward until the trench J.11 was captured; their first task was to bring oblique fire to bear on the trenches J.10 and J.11 so as to assist the Lancashire Fusiliers.

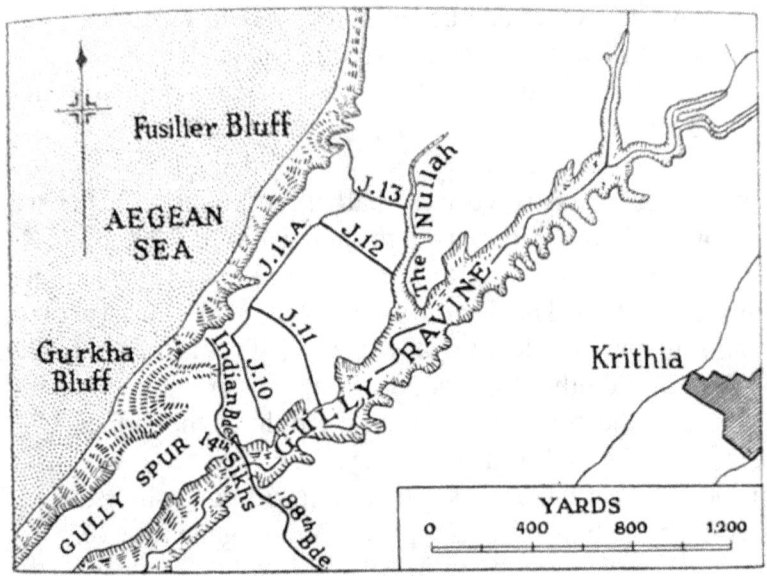

GALLIPOLI. THE GULLY RAVINE.
4th June, 1915.

In accordance with brigade orders, forty-five men, under a jemadar, were detailed to remain as garrison of the Battalion's original trenches. Every man taking part in the attack was to carry an entrenching tool tied to his back. There were six wire Cutters in each company, and these were distributed among men in the front rank. Grappling irons and planks were issued to Number 2 Double-Company to assist it in crossing the enemy's wire entanglement across the bottom of the ravine

Colonel Palin's written orders were issued in the evening of 3 June, but thorough preparations had by then been completed and everything was ready for next day's battle. There was a general feeling of optimism and the morale of the Battalion was very high.

The general course of the Third Battle of Krithia may be summarised in a few words. On both the Allied flanks the attack was a complete failure: in the centre, after preliminary success on a comparatively wide front, the final result was a gain of two hundred and fifty to five hundred yards of ground on a frontage of about a mile. The French on the right lost 2,000 casualties the British 4,500 out of a total of about 16,000 actually engaged. The Turkish losses are officially given as 9,000.

4 June was a beautiful summer day. To the front of the Indian Brigade the morning artillery bombardment took place according to the timetable previously arranged, but unfortunately produced little effect on the enemy in his strong trenches. The British were badly equipped with artillery; the proportion of howitzers was small, and there was very little high-explosive ammunition available. No howitzers had been allotted to assist the Indian Brigade and unfortunately at the last moment some of the field guns originally detailed to support it were diverted elsewhere. The result was that the garrisons of the Turkish trenches on Gully Spur were quite unshaken at zero hour.

Punctually at 12 noon the first wave of the Indian Brigade dashed forward to the attack. The Lancashire Fusiliers were mown down by fire on the very parapet of their trench; their attack was checked immediately; and throughout the day they were unable to make any progress. The failure in the centre reacted on the units on either flank. The 6th Gurkhas on the left gained some ground, but were forced eventually to withdraw to their original line. The fate of the 14th Sikhs on the right must be described in greater detail.

In the Gully Ravine Number 2 Double-Company, under Lieutenant Colonel Jacques, rushed forward with the utmost gallantry in face of a withering fire, mainly from machineguns in hidden positions on both banks of the ravine. The two British officers were killed, within a few minutes; the double-company nevertheless succeeded in forcing its way across an intact wire obstacle and in capturing a trench in the ravine. Wonderful resolution was displayed. At one spot, where heavy losses were being suffered whilst the men were trying to cut their way through wire, Havildar Maghar Singh[14] suddenly leapt the obstacle as if it were a hurdle and was followed immediately by his section. Number 2 Double-Company was almost annihilated.

On the right of Number 2, Number 4 Double-Company advanced from its trench extending for one hundred yards from the eastern edge of the ravine. It attempted to keep pace with the left of the 4th Worcestershire of the 88th Brigade. In this it was successful, but at heavy cost. On its front Number 4 had not such formidable opposition to encounter as had Number 2, but it suffered heavily from enfilade fire from the left – an enfilade fire from which the 88th Brigade was protected by the lie of the ground. Moreover, owing to the fact that the trench from which Number 4 issued to the attack lay obliquely to the line of advance, a number of men lost direction and, bearing too much to their left, became involved in the ravine itself. The double-company commander (Lieutenant Fowle) was killed and the other British officer (2nd Lieutenant Savory) wounded within the first five minutes. The double-company was reduced to a fraction in a very short time, but the remnants succeeded in gaining the enemy's front trench in conjunction with the left of the Worcesters. There they held on.

At 12:15 p.m. the second wave of attack dashed forward. On the left of the 14th Sikhs, Number 3 Double-Company advanced up the Gully Ravine, accompanied by Colonel Palin and battalion headquarters. They joined up with the remnants of Number 2 Double-Company. Then, seeing that further progress up the ravine was impossible owing to his left flank being exposed, Colonel Palin seized and occupied a narrow scar on the western edge, just south of the eastern end of the Turkish trench, J.10. Here, within a short time, Captain McRae (Commander of Number 3 Double-Company), Lieutenant Cremen (adjutant) and Lieutenant Meade (quartermaster) were all killed. In spite of heavy losses, however, the position gained was entrenched and held on to. During the afternoon the Battalion's two machineguns and also two machine

---

[14] In 1934 he was the Subadar Major of the Training Battalion and had been awarded the Order of British India.

guns of a naval armoured car section were brought forward to join Colonel Palin.

Meanwhile, on the right, Number 1 Double-Company under Captain Engledue, following in the wake of Number 4, had made a very fine advance. Keeping pace with the left of the Worcesters, it reached the enemy's third line of trenches. But by this time its strength had been reduced by casualties to Captain Engledue, Jemadar Narain Singh and about thirty men. This small party hung on in the captured trench for the rest of the day with difficulty keeping at bay bodies of Turks who attempted to bomb their way up from the Gully Ravine.[15] At about 6 p.m. the Worcesters, who earlier had got farther ahead were forced back and took position on Engledue's right. The Turks made no counterattack during the night, but early on the 5th started bombing attacks. A little later, when he received orders to withdraw, Engledue had only twelve effectives left with him.

During the afternoon of 4 June attempts were made to carry forward the attack of the Indian Brigade by means of reinforcements sent up from reserve. But no success whatever was attained.

All through the night Colonel Palin and his men, with extraordinary courage and resolution, held on under a murderous fire and in face of ever-increasing bombing attacks on their left flank from the higher ground. At daybreak on the 5th it was seen that the Turks were working round to the rear and that there was every chance of being surrounded. One of the 14th Sikhs machine guns had been destroyed by a bomb and the crews of both were almost all casualties. Both the naval guns had been knocked out during the night, and their commander was wounded. With Colonel Palin were only the Battalion medical officer (Lieutenant Cursetjee) and forty-seven men unwounded. It was therefore decided to withdraw. The retirement was carried out successfully and in good order.

---

[15] As the men of the 14th Sikhs had not been trained in the use of the bomb, each double-company in the attack on 4 June was accompanied by one or two British sappers carrying jam-tin bombs in a sandbag. All these sappers were soon killed; but some of the bombs were used by Engledue and his party.

Midday on 5 June found the remnants of the 14th Sikhs collected in their original trenches, whence they were sent back into reserve to rest and reorganise.

An act of ill-fated gallantry remains to be recorded. Lieutenant Mathew, the Battalion machinegun officer, had been kept back when his guns were taken forward to join Colonel Palin. On hearing that one of his guns, though undamaged, had perforce been abandoned, Mathew led a party to retrieve it. It was a forlorn hope. Though with great heroism Mathew and his men succeeded in reaching the gun, they could not bring it in. As each man carrying the gun was hit, another took his place. Finally Mathew alone was left unhurt. He picked up the gun and struggled with it a few yards until he too fell, hit in seven places. He was brought in eventually, but died later of his wounds in hospital at Alexandria.

The Losses of the 14th Sikhs on 4–5 June 1915

	British Officers	Indian Officers	Indian Other Ranks
Killed	9	3	134
Wounded	3	8	202
Missing (believed dead)			35
Total	**12**[16]	**11**	**371**

For various reasons, one Indian officer and over sixty other ranks did not participate in the attack. The strength of the Battalion actually engaged was 15 British officers (including the medical officer), 13 Indian officers and 450 Indian other ranks. The casualties therefore amounted to 82 percent of the men actually engaged. The only British officers left unwounded were Colonel Palin (who received three bullets through his headdress, but was

---

[16] Killed: Lieutenant Colonel F. A. Jacques; Captain A. W. McRae; Lieutenants L. R. Fowle, L. F. Cremen, R. J. F. P. Meade, H. E. Masters; 2nd Lieutenants G. W. Hornsby, W. H. Lowry, S. V. Hasluck.
Wounded: Lieutenant M. C. G. Mathew (mortally); 2nd Lieutenants R. A. Savory, R. G. Wreford.

untouched), Captain Engledue and the medical officer, Lieutenant Cursetjee.

The Third Battle of Krithia remains a glorious memory and inspiration: never has any battalion displayed finer devotion to duty. The splendid conduct of the 14th Sikhs did not escape notice. Writing to the Commander-in-Chief in India a few weeks after the event, General Sir Ian Hamilton paid noble tribute to the heroism of all ranks. Some passages from his letter (which was published in the Indian Press) may be quoted:

> In the highest sense of the word extreme gallantry has been shown by this fine Battalion. In spite of these tremendous losses there was not a sign of wavering all day. Not an inch of ground gained was given up and not a single straggler came back …. The ends of the enemy's trenches leading into the ravine were found[17] to be blocked with the bodies of Sikhs and of the enemy who died fighting at close quarters, and the glacis slope is thickly dotted with the bodies of these fine soldiers all lying on their faces as they fell in their steady advance on the enemy. The history of the Sikhs affords many instances of their value as soldiers but it may be safely asserted that nothing finer than the grim valour and steady discipline displayed by them on 4 June has ever been done by soldiers of the *Khalsa*. Their devotion to duty and their splendid loyalty to their orders and to their leaders make a record their nation should look back upon with pride for many generations.

The gallantry of the Regiment was also referred to by the Secretary of State for India (Mr Austen Chamberlain) in a moving speech in the House of Commons, and Mr Chamberlain personally attended a memorial service held in a London church for the fallen officers of the 14th Sikhs.

In India the news of the Battalion's heroism was received at a moment when subversive elements were doing their utmost to undermine the spirit of the Sikhs in the Punjab. Speaking two years

---

[17] i.e. after the successful British advance on 28 June 1915

later to an Indian audience at a Durbar at Ludhiana, Sir Michael O'Dwyer, Lieutenant-Governor of the Punjab, referred to the incipient disaffection in that province in the earlier months of 1915. After touching upon the great achievement of the 14th in Gallipoli, he said:

> It is an admitted fact that the Sikh spirit, instead of being daunted by that terrible sacrifice of Gallipoli, was roused to a higher pitch of martial ardour. I remember well that when news was made public numbers of my Sikh friends came to see me, not with sorrow but with a feeling of pride at the heroic sacrifice, and it is a matter of history that from that day the Sikh eagerness for recruiting received its strongest impetus.

For a short time after 5 June the shrunken 14th Sikhs remained in reserve, Colonel Palin was transferred temporarily to command the 126th Brigade, and Captain Engledue took over command of the Battalion. The 1/5th and 2/10th Gurkhas, who had recently arrived in Gallipoli, now replaced the two British battalions in the Indian Brigade, which thus once more comprised solely of Indian troops.

On 14 June the 14th Sikhs moved into the front line trenches on the right of the brigade line and remained there until the 23rd. This was a comparatively quiet period and only eight casualties were incurred, but so weak was the Battalion strength that every man was doing duty. The guard on the regimental dump was commanded by the carpenter, who had under him the regimental armourer and the regimental bootmaker! On the 23rd the Battalion, reinforced by a welcome draft of one hundred men from India, went back into reserve. Next day Colonel Palin rejoined.

By this time conditions at Helles were becoming increasingly unpleasant and depressing. The heat of the midday sun was intense; there was very little shade; the water supply was limited. The atmosphere was often thick with dense clouds of dust. A plague of large flies caused constant irritation to all and infection to many, and an epidemic of dysenteric diarrhoea was extremely prevalent. There continued to be the constant strain of never being safe from hostile shellfire.

CHAPTER 6
1915

THE GREAT WAR,

GALLIPOLI, 28 JUNE–14 December 1915

The battle of 4 June showed clearly that in the Helles area we did not possess sufficient howitzers to support a general attack all along the line. Further attempts to gain ground were therefore made by a succession of attacks on narrow fronts supported by massed artillery fire.

THE ACTION OF GULLY RAVINE, 28 June–5 July

An attack of this nature was carried out on 28 June on the left of the British line by the 29th Division and one brigade of the 52nd Division. Considerable success was gained. On Gully Spur five Turkish trench lines were captured, though the enemy soon regained the eastern portions of the two most northerly lines. The 14th Sikhs, numerically very weak, formed the reserve of the 29th Division and did not take part in the actual attack.

As soon as the first Turkish trench line had been captured, Sikh working parties began to dig a communication trench to join it up to our original line. The Battalion suffered a few casualties from shellfire, and Lieutenant Cursetjee, the medical officer, was wounded whilst attending to a private of the Royal Fusiliers who had been hit. Later in the day a shell burst over Colonel Palin, Captain Engledue and 2nd Lieutenant Savory as they were proceeding in single file along the newly-made communication trench. Colonel Palin was untouched, but Captain Engledue was seriously wounded and 2nd Lieutenant Savory slightly so.

On 29 June the 14th Sikhs, as reserve to the Indian Brigade, moved forward to a bivouac near the sea coast. That day, Colonel Palin was posted temporarily to the command of the 156th Brigade (52nd Division), and 2nd Lieutenant Savory took over command, being the only British officer left with the Battalion. For the next two days the 14th remained in reserve and were employed in improving a cart track along the narrow beach between the cliffs and the sea. The track was under hostile observation, and any movement along it by formed bodies of troops, or transport, came under immediate and accurate artillery fire. Casualties in the Battalion between 29 June and 1 July amounted to two men killed and seventeen wounded.

Soon after dawn on 2 July the 14th Sikhs moved up to the front line to relieve part of the 6th Gurkhas.

By this time the extreme left of the British line rested on a spur running down to the sea, later known as Fusilier Bluff, whence it extended for about two hundred yards inland along a former Turkish trench, J.13. The eastern portion of this trench, which led into 'The Nullah' – a tributary running southward into the Gully Ravine – was in Turkish hands. The easternmost point held by us in J.I3 was protected by a barricade and a machine gun, and from that point the British line ran southward along an old Turkish communication trench (J.11a). The portion of front line allotted to the 14th Sikhs included the angle where the line bent back and about one hundred yards on either side of it. Owing to the configuration of the ground, the troops holding the old Turkish communication trench could not fire into 'The Nullah', about two hundred yards to the east, which could thus be used by the enemy for the massing of men prior to an assault.

At 6 p.m. on 2 July, after a two hours' artillery bombardment, the Turks made a heavy attack against the head of the salient held by the Indian Brigade. The main weight of their effort fell against the trench line held by the 14th Sikhs and 6th Gurkhas. The attack was delivered across the open from dead ground only one hundred and fifty yards away; but no Turk succeeded in reaching our line. The enemy displayed great bravery and his casualties were very heavy. Within fifty yards of the British trench line was left a line of corpses which at night gave the impression of an enemy crawling forward and was responsible for more than one false alarm.

Shortly before 9 p.m. the enemy opened another bombardment which lasted for fifteen minutes. Supports of both 14th Sikhs and 6th Gurkhas were assembled in a depression about fifty yards behind the firing line. When the bombardment ceased as suddenly as it had begun, the supports rose as one man and in complete silence rushed up the slope to the firing trench, arriving on the parados just as the Turks emerged from cover to assault. There was insufficient room in the trench for them all and those that remained outside, both Sikhs and Gurkhas stood upon the parados and fired over the heads of their comrades. This spontaneous and entirely unrehearsed movement was, according to an eyewitness, a most impressive spectacle.

The enemy's second attack was not pressed with the vigour of the first and was repulsed without much difficulty. During the lull between the two attacks, Major H. G. Wilmer (staff captain of the Indian Brigade) rejoined and took over command of the 14th Sikhs. Casualties in the Battalion during the 2nd July were seven men killed and thirty wounded.

On 3 July orders were received to gain possession of the whole of the trench J.13, and preparations were made to this end. At 7 p.m. a party of Sikh bombers, together with three bombers each from the 5th and 6th Gurkhas, assembled under Major Wilmer at the British barricade. They pulled it down and advanced eastward along the trench, which was unoccupied up to a point where the enemy had a similar barricade. This was quickly reached and demolished; but it was found that the Turks had erected farther down the trench another barricade, from which a sharp fire was at once directed against Wilmer's small party. No less than five attempts were made to rush the enemy, but the resistance proved too strong. After about one and a half hours' bombing, the party was forced back to our line. Of the 14th Sikhs three men were killed, and two Indian officers and twenty-one other ranks wounded. This was the last attempt made to drive the Turks out of J.13 by direct attack, and the enemy remained in possession of the eastern end of that trench until the end of the Gallipoli campaign.

For the 14th Sikhs 4 July was a quiet day, marred by the melancholy spectacle of a large French transport torpedoed by a submarine. The whole affair was over in a couple of minutes. An explosion was followed by the rapid sinking of the stern of the ship, which stood on end, remained so poised for a few seconds, and then disappeared. Her disappearance was followed by great activity on the part of destroyers in the neighbourhood, while all the remaining transports weighed anchor and made off at full speed for the harbours of Mudros or Imbros.

Shortly before dawn on 5 July reports were passed along from the 6th Gurkhas, on the left of the 14th, that the enemy seemed to be preparing to attack. The warning was justified. At about 3 a.m. a strong attack developed. In the half-light of dawn, wave upon wave of Turks issued from dead ground, advanced fifty yards or so, and then melted away under our machinegun and rifle fire. The pressure was greatest on the Sikhs' right flank, where the Battalion linked up with the 10th Gurkhas; but the Turks gained no success. Under a murderous fire their advancing lines withered away. Our men, unshaken by any previous bombardment, were able to fire coolly and undisturbed at the enemy. Before long, our supporting artillery opened accurate fire on the enemy's assembly positions, and by 8:30 a.m. the Turkish effort was entirely spent. Once again the Turkish infantry had displayed extreme gallantry.

Casualties in the 14th Sikhs were Major Wilmer and Subadar Dhiyan Singh killed, four other ranks killed and twenty-four wounded.

Later in the day the Indian Brigade was relieved in the front line and went into bivouac on the sea coast. By this time the brigade had become a mere skeleton. The 1/5th and 1/6th Gurkhas had been temporarily amalgamated, and the 14th attached to the 2/10th Gurkhas for rations and maintenance. The 14th Sikhs had dwindled to a strength of one British officer (2nd Lieutenant Savory), one Indian officer (Subadar Major Sham Singh) and one hundred and seventeen other ranks. Like the 14th the 1/5 Gurkhas also had only one British officer left.

The eight days fighting at Helles ending on 5 July 1915 are officially entitled the Action of Gully Ravine. It is now known that the enemy's losses were even heavier than were estimated at the time – no less than sixteen thousand, of whom fourteen thousand fell in the struggle on both sides of the Gully Ravine. The Turks on the evening of 5 July were in no condition to withstand further attack. Fortunately for them, Sir Ian Hamilton had no reserves of men and ammunition at hand to exploit the situation.

5 July was destined to be the last day that the Indian Brigade was in action in the Helles area. A few days were spent in bivouac on the coast, and the brigade was then moved from the peninsula to the island of Imbros for rest and reorganisations. Embarking during the night of 10 July, the 14th Sikhs arrived at Kephalos Bay early on the 11th after a few hours' voyage.

IMBROS

The brigade bivouacked in a field about half a mile from the seashore. There for the first time for ten weeks the men could safely live above ground and walk about in the open. The change to peaceful and uncramped conditions benefited them both mentally and physically, and they revelled in long hours of sleep and almost unlimited facilities for bathing. Time was spent in 'smartening up' parades and field training. The Battalion won a bomb-throwing competition. Officers went on expeditions into the interior of Imbros Island and frequently visited Panaghyr, its pretty little Capital.

On 12 July the Battalion was reinforced by a double-company of the Patiala Imperial Service Infantry commanded by Major

Hardam Singh, with Captain A. F. MacLean and 2nd Lieutenant G. H. Whitfield as special service officers. The double-company was 'attached for operations only.' This meant that administration rested with the commander of the Patiala double-company as distinct from the commander of the 14th Sikhs – an arrangement which might have led to friction and duplication of work but for the cooperation of both parties. Later, the Patialas were incorporated into the Battalion as a fifth double-company.

Reinforcing drafts of officers and men arrived at intervals, while many who had been wounded, or invalided, rejoined. Colonel Palin returned to the Battalion on 18 July and had a great reception from all ranks. Another pre-war officer, Captain Daniell, also rejoined from France, where he had been serving with the 15th Sikhs.

As time went on signs were not lacking that the period of rest was drawing to a close. Conferences of commanding officers; staff tours to the peninsula; battalion and brigade night training operations; embarkation and disembarkation parades; all pointed to an early return to active service. Some British divisions had arrived from England and were also busy training.

ANZAC

The 14th Sikhs embarked in trawlers on 5 August for a destination which was kept secret. They arrived off Anzac at about 9 p.m. There was no mistaking the locality, even in the dark: a black mountainous mass rising out of the sea, silhouetted against the deep blue sky and twinkling with countless lights. All night long the trawlers lay out to sea. At daybreak on the 6th disembarkation was started. But, after half the 14th had got ashore, the Turks began to shell the beach heavily; and the other half-battalion was ordered to remain out at sea until dark. It spent an uncomfortable day, for the sea got up and the trawlers were tossed about like corks.

Sir Ian Hamilton's great offensive, for which plans and arrangements had been maturing for some time past, was now about to take place. Attacks were to be delivered in three localities on the Gallipoli peninsula – at Helles, at Anzac and at Suvla. The main effort was to be made from the Anzac position; and it was in this main effort that the 14th Sikhs, as part of the Indian Brigade, was to participate.

The Anzac position, facing eastward, formed a rough semicircle with the sea as its base. The Turkish line faced ours at close distance, but, unlike ours, its flanks did not rest on the sea; this had been prevented by stationing on either flank a British warship whose business it was to check any attempt by the enemy to prolong his line to the seashore.

THE BATTLE OF SARI BAIR

From Anzac the British objective was the capture of the crest of the Sari Bair Ridge. It was hoped to occupy this ridge before dawn on 7 August after a night advance round the northern flank of the Turkish position. With the Sari Bair crest in British hands the enemy's defences at Anzac would become untenable. The arrangements for the attack from Anzac were entrusted to General Birdwood, who divided the troops at his disposal into two portions –one to hold the existing Anzac position and to deliver attacks intended to divert the enemy's attention, the other to carry out the main attack against the Sari Bair.

The troops for the main attack were placed under Major General Godley, commanding the New Zealand and Australian Division. He organised his force in four portions: a Right Covering Force, a Left Covering Force, a Right Assaulting Column and a Left Assaulting Column. The mission of the two covering forces was to clear the nearer foothills of the enemy so that the progress of the assaulting columns should not be delayed at the outset. It was hoped that the covering forces would be in occupation of their objectives before the assaulting columns began their advance. The Right Assaulting Column was to gain the Chunuk Bair Peak on the Sari Bair ridge; the Left Assaulting Column was to secure Hill Q and Koja Chemen Tepe, two peaks farther to the north-east.

The Left Assaulting Column had the more arduous task, as it had a much greater distance to traverse. And here mention must be made of the extreme difficulty of the country. The western side of the Sari Bair ridge slopes down in a tangled network of twisting spurs and ravines, rugged and steep and covered thickly with prickly scrub. There were no paths or tracks. The available maps were neither full nor accurate, and even the local guides who led the columns had little real knowledge of the ground. The 14th Sikhs formed part of the Left Assaulting Column (Brigadier General H. V. Cox), which consisted of the 4th Australian Brigade, Indian Brigade, 21st Indian Mountain Battery (less one section) and a field company of New Zealand Engineers.

Detailed orders and instructions for the column were issued during 6 August. No animals other than gun mules were to accompany units. The men would be heavily laden; for, though greatcoats and packs were not to be taken, every man would carry two hundred rounds of ammunition, his light entrenching tool, two empty sandbags and one day's cooked ration in addition to the emergency ration, while one man in every four was also to carry either a pick or a shovel. The head of the column (4th Australian Brigade) was to march out of the northern end of the Anzac defences at 9:45 p.m. The 14th Sikhs were to bring up the rear and to detach one double-company as escort to the mountain guns.

The route to be taken led northwards for about a mile along the rough track near the sea coast to the mouth of the ravine known as Aghyl Dere, and thence eastward up the ravine. The advance up the ravine would be protected on its left, or northern, flank by the Left Covering Force in position on Damakjelik Bair. After working up the Aghyl Dere for some distance, it was intended to divide the Left Assaulting Column into two portions – one to advance on Hill Q and the other to move via the Abdul Rahman spur on Koja Chemen Tepe.

The total distance to be covered by the column was about three miles, and it was hoped that the summit of the Sari Bair ridge would be gained by 3 a.m. But, as the Official Historian points out, the calculations were too optimistic: 'Apart from the chance of opposition, they made an insufficient allowance for the checks and delays inseparable from a night march through amazingly difficult country, culminating in a steep climb up a rugged hill which had never been reconnoitred.'

Actually, the head of the 4th Australian Brigade did not leave the starting point till after 11 p.m., and progress was so slow that the double-company of Sikhs at the rear of the column did not move forward till nearly 4 a.m. on 7 August. (The 14th were only two double-companies strong, not having yet been joined by the half-battalion left out at sea during the 6th; and one double-company, as already mentioned, had been detached as escort to the mountain battery.)

The main reason for this most unfortunate delay was that terrible snare, the 'short cut.' The officer leading the column was persuaded by the native guide accompanying him to leave the coastal track earlier than had been intended, so as to reach the Aghyl Dere by a short cut through a narrow gorge. The gorge was in fact, only six hundred yards long, but was so overgrown with scrub that engineers had to be sent forward to clear a way for troops. Further, the column was sniped at from both flanks, probably only a few Turkish scouts were present but they delayed progress most effectively. The night was pitch black, there was considerable confusion and disorder. The head of the column took three hours to get through the gorge.

7 August

By daybreak (about 4:30 a.m.) the leading Australian troops had reached a point on the Damakjelik spur less than a mile eastward of the mouth of the Aghyl Dere. Apart from occasional sniping, Turkish opposition had ceased. But the Australians were absolutely exhausted and unable to go further. They were ordered to dig in where they were. The three Gurkha battalions of the Indian Brigade had moved off to the south-east in the direction of Hill Q. In an astoundingly intricate country they had great difficulty in maintaining direction and became somewhat scattered. The 6th Gurkhas reached a point west of Hill Q from which that eminence (not as yet occupied by the enemy) could have been reached in an hour's climb; but the battalion was isolated and an order reached it to dig in where it was and renew the attack the next day.

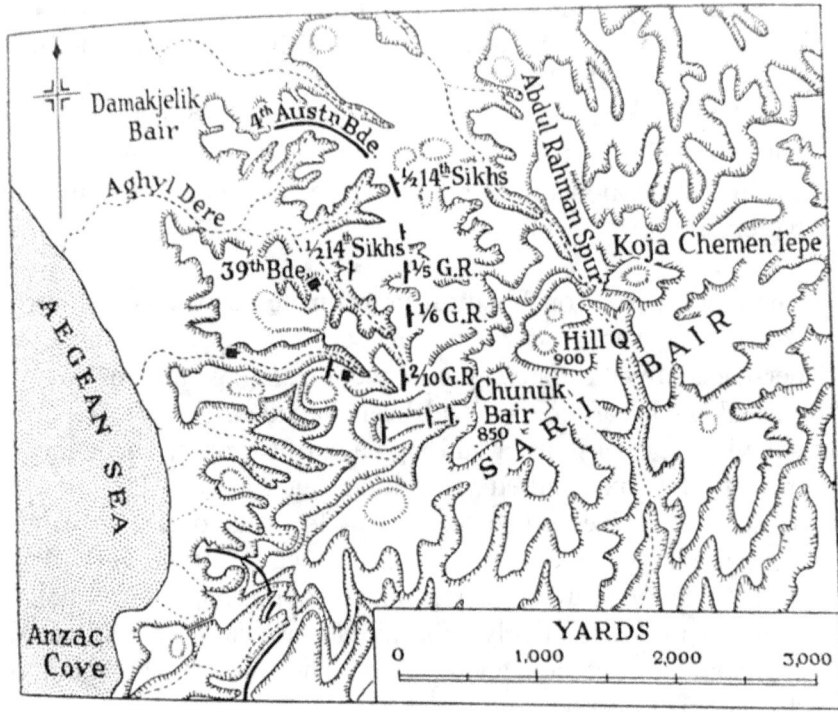

GALLIPOLI. BATTLE OF SARI BAIR.
Evening, 7th August, 1915.

It was broad daylight when Colonel Palin, having with him only one double-company of the 14th Sikhs, reached General Cox's headquarters in the Aghyl Dere. By 8:30 a.m. Colonel Palin had joined the headquarters of the 5th Gurkhas, who were occupying a line, astride a ravine, about twelve hundred yards north-west of Hill Q. The Gurkhas were in touch with the enemy on a wide front and had suffered a number of casualties. Captain Daniell, with thirty Sikhs, was sent to reinforce a somewhat isolated Gurkha double-company on the extreme left of the line. His small detachment was under fire all day and suffered a considerable percentage of casualties.

At about 10:30 a.m. Colonel Palin was instructed that Brigadier General Cayley with the 39th Brigade would shortly arrive, and that the 5th Gurkhas and 14th Sikhs would then advance in conjunction with the 39th Brigade to capture Koja Chemen Tepe. However, this plan did not materialise and no further advance was made during the day.

The double-company of the 14th which had been detached as escort to the mountain battery rejoined battalion headquarters in the afternoon. The two double-companies which had been unable to disembark the previous day joined Colonel Palin at 7 p.m. One of them (the Patiala double-company) was sent to join Captain Daniell, who had during the afternoon been reinforced by the remainder of his own double-company.

Casualties in the 14th Sikhs on 7 August totalled about fifty, including 2nd Lieutenant Reeves wounded. They were all incurred by the party on the left of the 5th Gurkhas' line

7 August, the first day of the Battle of Sari Bair, ended without any British success being achieved. Like General Cox's column, the Right Assaulting Column also failed to gain the summit of the Sari Bair ridge, either before dawn, as planned, or later during the day. By evening the advantage of surprise was lost, and it was obviously only a question of time before the Turks brought up reinforcements to the threatened points. However, hope of ultimate success was not yet abandoned and orders were issued for a general assault at dawn on the 8th against Chunuk Bair, Hill Q and Koja Chemen Tepe.

General Cox now had thirteen battalions at his disposal, though they were scattered over a wide front. He organised his force in four columns. Their various objectives were: Number 1 Column (the most southerly) – the northern slopes of Chunuk Bair; Number 2 –the southern peak of Hill Q: Number 3 – the northern peak of Hill Q: Number 4 – Abdul Rahman spur and Koja Chemen Tepe. Number 3 Column, under Colonel Palin, comprised the 14th Sikhs and 1/5th Gurkhas. Number 4 Column consisted of the 4th Australian Brigade and 6th King's Own Regiment.

Though warned on the evening of the 7th that the attack would be resumed next morning, General Cox's actual operation order did not reach Colonel Palin until 2 a.m. on 8 August. Colonel Palin's orders were then issued verbally to the commander of the 5th Gurkhas, and a written copy was conveyed personally by Lieutenant Savory (adjutant) to the two double-companies of the 14th Sikhs on the left of the line which were now under the command of Captain Maclean. Savory had nearly half a mile to traverse through thick scrub and across the steep sides of a ravine, and did not reach MacLean's headquarters till 3:30 a.m.

The advance was due to start at 4:15 a.m. The 5th Gurkhas were to move forward straight to their front. MacLean's half-battalion of Sikhs would, in its advance attempt to outflank the enemy facing the Gurkhas. Half the 14th were to form Colonel Palin's reserve.

8 August

The advance began, as planned, at 4:15 a.m. It was immediately opposed in strength, and no success was attained. The Gurkhas were unable to gain any ground at all. On the left MacLean's two double-companies succeeded in getting forward some three hundred yards to the edge of a ravine, with precipitous sides, running at right angles to the line of advance. There they were held up by heavy machinegun fire. Before long, the right of the 4th Australian Brigade came up on the left of the Sikhs. A little later, the left flank of the Australians was driven back in confusion by a Turkish counterattack. By 8:30 a.m. all the Australians and also the two Sikh double-companies were forced back to the positions from which they had started.

Of the 14th Sikhs' half-battalion only sixty-nine effectives remained. The casualties were: Killed: Captain A. F. MacLean, 2nd Lieutenant G. H. Whitfield, Subadar Jaimal Singh (of the Patiala double-company) and 14 other ranks; Wounded: Captain J. A. S. Daniell, Captain M. Saunders, Major Hardam Singh (of the Patiala double-company), one Indian officer and 134 other ranks.

No further attempt to advance could be made by Number 3 Column without reinforcements, and there were none available. The other columns under General Cox were equally unsuccessful. The only success attained during 8 August was farther south, where a precarious footing was gained on Chunuk Bair.

9 August

On 9 August a further attempt was made to gain the Sari Bairi ridge, but once more in vain. Only a portion of General Cox's troops participated in the attacks, and the 14th Sikhs were not engaged therein. The battalion however did not have an entirely peaceful day and suffered about thirty casualties including Major F.A. London wounded. In the early morning the 4th Australian Brigade on Damakjelik spur was heavily counter attacked, but succeeded in driving back the enemy with loss. In the evening General Cox withdrew the 14th Sikhs into reserve.

10 August

Next morning at 5 a.m. the Battalion was sent forward again to reinforce the 5th Gurkhas, and remained all day in position on their right. It was not seriously engaged, however, and suffered only a few casualties. 10 August – the concluding day of the Battle of Sari Bair – was marked by desperate fighting further south in the vicinity of Chunuk Bair, where a strong Turkish counterattack drove back our troops which had gained a footing on the top.

The casualties in the 14th Sikhs between 7 and 11 August totalled:
    Killed: 2 British officers, 1 Indian officer, 20 other ranks.
    Wounded: 3 British officers, 6 Indian officers, 227 other ranks
The number of effectives at Colonel Palin's disposal on the evening of the 11th was 6 British officers, 1 Indian officer and 223 other ranks.

We have described briefly the part played by one battalion in the great battle that raged over the Gallipoli peninsula between 7 and

10 August. There has been no attempt to cover the whole area concerned; and little if any reference has been made to the bitter fighting at Helles or in the vicinity of the main Anzac position, or to the melancholy series of events at Suvla. Sir Ian Hamilton's venture failed, but it went very near to success. The reasons for failure need not be discussed here.

After 10 August the Indian Brigade formed part of the garrison of the northern portion of the extended Anzac position. Until 20 August the brigade was mainly employed in digging by night, a defensive position on the Damakjelik spur. There was no serious fighting during this period, but a slow wastage of men from wounds, or sickness, was continuous. Between 11 and 20 August the 14th Sikhs had one man killed and twenty-one wounded. A draft consisting of Major Earle, Captain Finnis, two Indian officers and one hundred and thirty-eight other ranks joined the Battalion on the 12th.

The Battalion was not one of the units employed in the desperate attacks on Hill 60 that took place between 21 August and the end of the month. Though not actively engaged, it suffered thirty casualties on the 21st and 22nd. Colonel Palin was invalided on 29 August, and the command of the 14th Sikhs devolved on Major E. S. Earle, who was granted the temporary rank of lieutenant colonel on 28 September 1915.

From the beginning of September onwards operations settled down into the regular routine of trench warfare. There were no further attacks on a large scale. The Indian Brigade held a front on the extreme left flank of the Anzac defences, extending northward from Hill 60 and joining up with the right of IX Corps at Suvla. The whole line was quickly converted into a strong trench system.

Colonel Palin returned from sick leave on 25 September and took over command of the Indian Brigade. (General Cox had previously been invalided to England.) About the same time the brigade was strengthened by the arrival of the 1/4th Gurkhas from France.

Casualties in the 14th Sikhs:

	Killed	Wounded
September	3	13
October	8	32
November	4	33

On 19 September a small transport, the S.S. *Ramzan*, carrying Indian drafts, was torpedoed and sunk in the Mediterranean by a submarine. Second Lieutenant C. J. Unger and eighty men of the 14th Sikhs were drowned; 2nd Lieutenant A. J. M. Reeves and thirty-four men were among the survivors who managed to escape in boats to an island whence, after suffering much hardship, they were taken away on 4 October by ship to Malta.

On 16 September the Battalion was reinforced by a strong draft of the 87th Punjabis under Captain V. Coates. For a time it was kept intact and formed into a fifth double-company.

On 1 October a second double-company, a double-company of Patiala Imperial Service Infantry joined the 14th Sikhs. It was commanded by Major Ishar Singh, with Major H. Campbell and 2nd Lieutenant P. S. Clarke as special service officers The Battalion was now reorganised into four double-companies as follows:

A and B Companies and 87th Punjabis detachment	Formed	Number 1 Double-Company Captain Coates
C and D Companies and one Patiala double-company	Formed	Number 2 Double-Company 2nd Lieutenant Clarke
E, F, G and H Companies	Formed	No 3 Double-Company Captain Finnis
One Patiala double-company	formed	Number 4 Double-Company Major Campbell

On 31 October there arrived a draft of 2 British officers, 6 Indian officers and 219 other ranks (including 4 Indian officers and 199 other ranks of the Burma Military Police).

The weather in November was delightful until the 26th, when a great storm burst over the Gallipoli peninsula. It has been described vividly in Masefield's *Gallipoli*:

> The 26th began as a cold, dour Gallipoli day with a bitter north-east wind, which increased in the afternoon to a fresh gale with sleet. Later it increased still more, and then blew hard, with thunder; and with the thunder came a rain more violent than any men of our army had ever seen. Water pours off very quickly from that land of abrupt slopes. In a few minutes every gully was a raging torrent and every trench a river.... At dark the sleet increased, the mud froze.... Before the night fell many of our men were frost-bitten.... The gale increased slowly all through the night, blowing hard and steadily from the north. At dawn it grew colder and the sleet hardened into snow, with an ever-increasing wind. The water from the flood had fallen in the night, but it was still four feet deep in many of the trenches. All through the 27th the wind gathered, till it was blowing a full gale, vicious and bitter cold: and on the 28th it reached its worst.... On the 29th the limits of human strength were reached.... The water fell during this day, but it left about two and a half feet of thick slushy mud.... After this the weather was fine and warm.[18]

The Indian Brigade, located on low ground, suffered at least its full share of hardships. The trenches acted as water conduits so that the rain which fell in the higher portions of the line was drained into the trench system lower down. Like a tidal wave, the water came rushing along the trenches, swirling into dug outs and round corners, carrying all before it. The sides of trenches were undercut and in many cases collapsed. Men were left standing waist deep in muddy water. In the 14th Sikhs' Officers' Mess dugout the water was level with the top of the table. It was impossible to light fires

---

[18] John Masefield, *Gallipoli* (London: Macmillan, 1916).

or cook for four days. The men's rations were ruined. All they had was a few biscuits.

The ensuing frost caused many casualties, particularly to those units in the front line. In the Suvla area the blizzard was responsible for over five thousand cases of frostbite, and more than two hundred men were drowned or frozen to death. Fortunately for the 14th, they were in reserve trenches. The men had their boots off, and therefore did not suffer so severely from trench feet as did some other units. There were only eighteen cases of frostbite in the Battalion. Even so, the men endured much hardship. Their spirit throughout was splendid. On the morning of the 28th the telephone orderly was found frozen to death at his post in the small dugout next to that of Colonel Earle. With the passing of the blizzard, the normal routine of trench warfare was resumed.

The first definite orders in regard to the evacuation of the peninsula reached the 14th Sikhs on 12 December. On the morning of the 14th the Sikhs were relieved in front line by the 4th Gurkhas. In the evening the Battalion filed past the starting point at brigade headquarters and took its place in a column which was moving towards the beach. The column moved single file quietly and without hurry.

In passing by the dumps and depots of Anzac, their deserted, almost desolate appearance struck the imagination. Former centres of feverish activity were silent as the grave. Scarcely anyone was met. Most of the troops still remaining were required in front line. But the beach was different. There, all was bustle and activity, though quiet and well ordered. The embarkation arrangements were admirable. With scarcely a check the Battalion filed on to a pier and thence were shipped into two lighters. These were ferried out to two small steamers, in which the Battalion sailed for Mudros about midnight.

At Mudros on the 15th the Battalion was transhipped into two large transports. These remained in harbour for another four days, taking in additional troops to their utmost capacity. On the 19th both ships sailed as part of a convoy for Alexandria, which was reached on the 22nd. The 14th Sikhs disembarked and entrained for Suez.

The casualties of the 14th Sikhs at Gallipoli amounted in all to:

	British Officers	Indian Officers	Indian Other Ranks
Killed	15	5	264
Wounded	12	11	840
Drowned	1	1	80
Invalided (including those who rejoined)			379

Every British officer who landed with the Battalion on 1 May was either killed or wounded. The strength of the Battalion on 15 December 1915 was 11 British officers[19] and 541 Indian ranks.

In concluding this Chapter, reference is due to the excellent service rendered by Sub-Assistant Surgeon Jemadar Bhagwan Singh. After Lieutenant Cursetjee had been wounded on 28 June, Jemadar Bhagwan Singh carried on medical duties with the Battalion single-handed for some time, and at Anzac he attended to other cases in addition to those of his own unit. He received a well-merited Indian Order of Merit (2nd Class) at the end of the Dardanelles campaign.

---

[19] Lieutenant Colonel E. S. Earle, Major H. Campbell (Guides), Captain H.C. Finnis, Captain V. Coates (87th Punjabis), 2nd Lieutenants R. A. Savory, C. A. Dunning, C. A. Keatinge, N. C. Wimbush, C. A. Maer, P. S. Clarke and Captain P. Connellan I.M.S. (medical officer)

CHAPTER 7
THE GREAT WAR:
1916–1918
EGYPT, BUSHIRE AND MESOPOTAMIA

After the evacuation of Gallipoli, the 29th Indian Infantry Brigade concentrated at Suez. The 14th Sikhs arrived there two days before Christmas, 1915, and went into camp on the outskirts of the town.

Early in 1916 a new formation, the 10th Indian Division was organised. This included the 29th Brigade, which was allotted to the southern sector of the Suez Canal defences.

The 14th Sikhs remained concentrated at Suez for a month. During this peaceful period opportunity was taken to reorganise, to revive physical fitness and to smarten up generally. The Battalion was brought up to full establishment by further drafts, including more men from the Burma Military Police and a complete company from the 82nd Punjabis. A number of officers and men who had been invalided from Gallipoli also rejoined.

On 9 January 1916 the Patiala troops serving with the Battalion left to rejoin their own unit. Their departure caused genuine regret. A fine body of men, their behaviour in action, their discipline and their cheerfulness had evoked general admiration. The 14th Sikhs were now reorganised as follows:

No 1 Double-Company	A and B Companies became A Company 87th Punjabis detachment became B Company
No 2 Double-Company	No change C Company D Company
No 3 Double-Company	E and F Companies became E Company G and H Companies became F Company
No 4 Double-Company	New drafts became G Company 82nd Punjabi detachment became H Company

At the same time the four-company and platoon organisation was adopted for training and tactical purposes, though not for administration. This was not a satisfactory arrangement, but it was sometime longer before the four-company organisation was adopted for all purposes in the Indian infantry.

On 23 January the 14th Sikhs moved from Suez to El Kubri, on the eastern bank of the canal. There, during the first half of February, the Battalion was employed in part of digging a new defence line east of the canal and also in preparing a cut for a pipe line to convey drinking water from Suez to the defences. On 13 February a detachment of two hundred men, under Captain Coates, was moved by sea to Abu Zenima, a port on the eastern shore of the Gulf of Suez. On the 14th, the remainder of the Battalion marched to El Shatt.

Before the end of February battalion headquarters were back again at Suez and on the 28th left that place by sea to garrison Tor and Abu Zenima, on the eastern side of the Gulf of Suez, in relief of Egyptian troops. Captain Coates's detachment already at Abu Zenima was increased to a strength of two double-companies (Numbers 2 and 3) and two machineguns. Battalion headquarters, with Numbers 1 and 4 Double-Companies and two machineguns, proceeded to Tor.

TOR

Tor was a quarantine station for pilgrims arriving from Mecca on their way to Egypt. There are a few fishing villages on the seashore. Landward, the country is arid desert. A priest of the Greek Church Monastery of St Katherine on Mount Sinai occupied a house close by. Tor might be described as the base for the monastery – and the priest a picturesque old fellow with his tall hat, long black robes and uncut hair – as the base commandant. All requirements for the monastery were sent up to Mount Sinai by caravan from Tor. The monastery is revered by Christians and Moslems alike, and its inhabitants are never molested by the Arabs. There is a legend that Mahomet himself slept the night there and was hospitably entertained and that as a mark of his appreciation, he commanded his followers always to treat the monastery with respect.

All ranks of the Regiment enjoyed their stay at Tor. It was a haven of rest, peaceful and extremely comfortable. The quarantine station, closed down for the War, had most up-to-date arrangements for treating and accommodating the pilgrims. The Sikhs were housed in barracks of palatial dimensions, and each building contained about twenty long baths and shower-baths with water laid on; the men spent most of their spare time washing. The Officers' Mess was established on the outskirts of the settlement in a villa built and furnished on the most modern lines, with a pleasant little garden.

The weather during March and April was delightful; cool cloudless days and cold nights. About a mile away there was a warm, slightly sulphurous spring which flowed into an old marble bath; here the officers bathed. The sea fishing was good, and officers also did a good deal of sailing in a hired dhow. They procured a rowing-boat, too, which was manned by sepoys. The standard of rowing was not high, but the men enjoyed the novelty

Occasional visits were made to Tor by H.M.S. *Fox* and a vessel in the Egyptian coastguard service. Rations, stores and mails were brought weekly by steamer from Suez. Battalion headquarters were in communication direct with IX Corps Headquarters at Suez by wireless.

The Turks had established posts in the foothills about ten miles to the east. Although the probability of hostile attack was not great, the necessary precautions had to be taken, local defences were reconstructed thoroughly. An observation post was established on a knoll four miles east of Tor, and mounted patrols were sent out at irregular intervals along all possible lines of approach. The Battalion was supplied with a number of riding camels for reconnaissance purposes, and the improvised camelry were further supplemented by an improvised troop of mounted infantry formed by mounting men on the officers' chargers. (Some of the Burma Military Police drafted into the Battalion were ex-cavalrymen.)

On 25 April the 14th Sikhs were relieved at Tor and Abu Zenima by the 23rd Sikh Pioneers, and returned to Suez. On 10 May the Battalion, together with the 2/10th Gurkhas, embarked under sealed orders in the transport *Ekma*. The *Ekma* touched at Aden five days later, and there it was learnt that the destination of the 14th was Bushire, on the southern coast of Persia. Bushire was reached on the evening of 21 May, disembarkation taking place next day.

BUSHIRE

Early in the War a number of German emissaries had entered Persia with the object of stirring up trouble for Britain in the East. They were bold and active, and attained a certain measure of success. The Persian Government being powerless to restrain them, the British were forced to take countermeasures. Throughout the War, British troops garrisoned the Bushire peninsula. In 1916 the Bushire garrison formed part of the Mesopotamia Expeditionary Force. The 14th Sikhs on arrival relieved the 96th Infantry (who went on to Mesopotamia)

The 14th remained at Bushire until February 1917. This period of eight months may be dismissed in a few words. The Bushire garrison had to take precautions against possible attack by Persian tribesmen from the hinterland. After May 1916, however, no such attack materialised and life for the garrison was peaceful and rather monotonous. At the end of 1916 the garrison consisted of one squadron 15th Lancers, the 14th Sikhs, 22nd Punjabis and nine guns of various sorts.

MESOPOTAMIA, 1917

On 6 February 1917 orders were received at Bushire for the 14th Sikhs to be prepared to leave immediately for the Tigris front.

At this period General Maude was conducting the series of successful operations – known officially as the Battle of Kut al Amara, 1917–which finally resulted in the defeat of the Turks on the Tigris, the pursuit of the enemy to Baghdad and the capture of Baghdad itself. There was hard fighting, for the Turks defended most stubbornly their entrenched positions on the south bank of the river about Kut. On 1 February 37th Brigade of the 14th Division was heavily engaged. Two of its battalions, the 36th and 45th Sikhs, that day gained great glory but at the same time suffered such crippling losses that it was necessary to withdraw them from the front to reorganise. Two other battalions were required to fill their places in the 37th Brigade, and the 14th Sikhs were one of those selected.

The Battalion embarked on 8 February in the transport *Bamora*, which sailed the same evening. There is only an open roadstead at Bushire, and the *Bamora* had to lie some miles off shore. Men, animals and stores were conveyed out to her in boats and lighters. Sixteen lighters were used, each of which could carry sixty men with their kits. Embarkation began at 8:30 a.m. and was completed by 3:30 p.m. The embarkation strength of the Battalion, under Lieutenant Colonel Earle, was 14 British officers, 16 Indian officers, one sub-assistant surgeon, 803 Indian other ranks and 58 followers. One Indian officer and nineteen other ranks were left behind at Bushire in hospital.

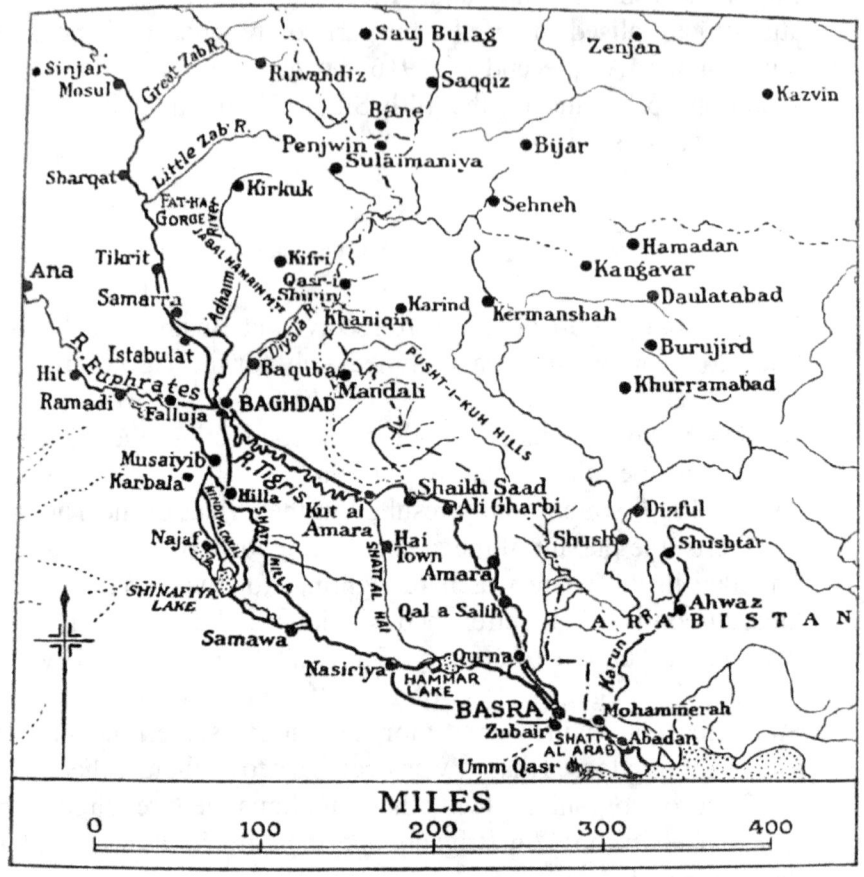

MESOPOTAMIA. 1917-1918.

The *Bamora* arrived at Basra on the evening of 9 February. Fresh posting orders were now received. The 14th Sikhs were to move up the Tigris for attachment to the 1st Corps in relief of the 2/9th Gurkhas, who were to join the 37th Brigade. This was a disappointment, as all ranks were looking forward to joining a brigade which included two other Sikh battalions, of whose withdrawal they were as yet unaware. The change in orders was due to a warning received by General Maude from India that heavy casualties in the 14th Sikhs could not be made by drafts. He was therefore constrained not to utilise the Battalion in the front line if possible. The Regiment was still maintained with a class composition entirely of Sikhs. Recruitment of Sikhs in India continued to prosper; but the drain on Sikh resources was immense.

The whole of 10 February was spent in transferring men, kit and stores to the river steamer *P.51* and two barges for the journey up the Tigris –a tedious business that was not completed till after dark. By February 1917 the Mesopotamia Force was well provided with river craft, and *P.51* was one of the best boats. A steamer travelling on the Tigris always had a barge, or lighter, lashed on either side of her. Not only did this arrangement increase the vessel's carrying capacity, but the barges were useful as buffers to the ship in the constant bumps against the banks that were unavoidable when navigating the more tortuous portions of the river.

The *P.51*, with her attendant barges, started from Basra at 10 p.m. on the 10th. The voyage of two hundred and sixty miles upriver was not uncomfortable, though devoid of special incident. Arab Village was reached on the evening of 13 February, and the 14th Sikhs disembarked next day.

Arab Village at this time was the British riverhead on the Tigris. There were camps and large quantities of stores on both banks of the river, which was spanned by a bridge of boats. On the north, or left bank, a defile, never more than a mile wide, extended between the Tigris and the great Suwaikiya marsh. Heavy fighting had taken place in this defile during the early months of 1916, and the Turks still held their formidable lines of trenches at Sannaiyat, five or six miles west of Arab Village. The other end of the defile was at Hanna, a few miles to the east.

The general position of the British and Turkish armies was curious. At Sannaiyat the Turks held the western end of the defile, facing east; and thence westward the enemy's line ran back along the Tigris's northern bank, facing south, as far as a point well upstream of Kut – a total stretch of twenty miles as the crow flies. General Maude confronted the Turks at Sannnaiyat on the north bank, and on the south bank his battle front extended from opposite Sannaiyat all along the south bank of the river well to the west of Kut. About Kut on the south bank were the British III Corps (13th and 14th Divisions), Cavalry Division and part of the 3rd Division of I

Corps. The remainder of the 3rd Division held the river line back to a point opposite Sannaiyat. The 7th Division of I Corps was on the north bank facing the enemy at Sannaiyat at very short distance.

On arriving at Arab Village on 13 February the 14th Sikhs became Corps troops under Major General Sir A. Cobbe, commander of I Corps. The Battalion took duties from the 2/9th Gurkhas. Two days later it relieved a battalion of the 7th Division in the Hanna piquet line, which protected the rear of the troops on the north bank of the Tigris against marauding Arabs.

The concluding phase of the long drawn-out Battle of Kut al Amara began on 22 February, when the 7th Division assaulted the Sannaiyat position and gained a large measure of success. Next morning, troops of the III Corps successfully effected a crossing of the Tigris to the west of Kut, whereupon the whole Turkish Army retreated on Baghdad.

On 24 February the 14th Sikhs were placed at the disposal of the 7th Division, but remained on duty at Arab Village. Two days later, the Battalion was transferred to the line of communication defences, which were quickly extended up the river as General Maude pressed on towards Baghdad. The 14th now became a unit of Number 3 Section of the Tigris Defences, and there ensued a long period of monotonous, though essential, duty on the line of communication.

During March the Battalion was distributed with headquarters and one company at Arab Village (south bank), one company in a line of blockhouses which were constructed on the Hanna piquet line, and two companies in a series of posts on the north bank from Sannaiyat westwards.[20] Early in the month the clearance of the Sannaiyat battlefield was carried out. This was an unpleasant task not unattended by danger, as many unexploded bombs were lying about. One day the gruesome discovery was made in a trench dugout of a deserted Turkish field ambulance in which each bed

---

[20] As previously mentioned, the large company subdivided into four platoons had for some time past been organised for tactical purposes, though not as yet for administration. It was finally adopted for all purposes in August 1917.

contained a dead body. Arab looters and marauders were troublesome at first, but their activities were soon suppressed by the alertness and good shooting of the Sikhs.

In April there was a readjustment of the various battalion posts, which by this time extended from below Arab Village up to Kut. Battalion headquarters remained at Arab Village. From April onwards the local Arabs became quite friendly, and but little trouble was experienced with rifle thieves and marauders. This was undoubtedly due to the revival of British prestige owing to our victories and capture of Baghdad. The state of affairs had been very different in 1916 after the fall of Kut.

At the end of April the hot weather began to make itself felt. During May it was hot by day, but the nights were quite cool and there was generally a breeze blowing. In June also the heat was not unbearable. The health of the 14th Sikhs was good throughout. Although the early summer of 1917 was cooler than the similar period in 1916, this alone does not account for the marked improvement in the health of the British Army in Mesopotamia. In 1917 the army was well found, well equipped and well fed; above all, its morale was very high.

Early in June the Battalion machine-gunners were withdrawn to Amara to join the newly-formed Number 1 Indian Machine Gun Company. They did not rejoin the Regiment till 1919. At the end of June the 14th were concentrated at Kut preparatory to leaving the lines of communication for the front. The first fortnight of July was a most uncomfortable time owing to a spell of terrific heat. Daily shade temperatures of 127 degrees F. were not unusual. The dust was incredible.

On 13 July the Battalion left Kut by river steamer for Baghdad, distant by water two hundred and thirteen miles. Navigation on this stretch was difficult owing to the many bends of the river, and at this season was further impeded by shoals with shallow and winding channels. The voyage up river was consequently slow. For the night of the 13th the steamer stopped at Bughaila, a line of communication post which was garrisoned by the 45th Sikhs, and did not sail again till late next morning. This gave an opportunity for fraternisation with the 45th which was not neglected.

The 14th disembarked at the Baghdad 'advanced base' on the Tigris's right bank, some miles below the town, on 17 July. Next day they moved camp to a palm grove higher up the river near the headquarters of the 3rd Division, to which the Battalion was now attached. The British officers established their Mess in a house on the river bank, and were fortunate enough to find within the enclosure of the building a well from which ice-cold water was obtainable.

At the end of July the Battalion was ordered to Falluja, on the Euphrates, some forty miles west of Baghdad. In view of the great heat and lack of water on the route, the move was carried out in two night marches. Starting at 7 p.m. on the 28th, the 14th Sikhs arrived at Nukhta at 5 a.m. next morning. This march of twenty-four miles was extremely trying, owing to clouds of dust and a following breeze. Falluja was reached at dawn on the 30th, and the Battalion came under the orders of the 7th Infantry Brigade.

During the summer of 1917 the frontage maintained by General Maude to cover Baghdad lay roughly on an arc of a circle, the centre of which was at Baghdad with radii extending north-east, north and west. The advanced British position in the centre was at Samarra on the Tigris. The British left flank lay at Falluja. The Turks had retired beyond close striking distance, and their strength was considerably inferior to that at General Maude's disposal. It was anticipated, however, that the enemy would be reinforced and attempt to take the offensive in the autumn.

The 7th Infantry Brigade was withdrawn from Falluja to the Baghdad area during August, and a new formation, the 50th Infantry Brigade, came into being. This included the 6th Jats, 14th Sikhs, 24th Punjabis and 97th Infantry. Brigadier General Andrew arrived at Falluja on 22 August to assume command of the 50th Brigade and of the Falluja area.

In September the 6th Cavalry Brigade and the bulk of 15th Division were concentrated at Falluja for operations against the Turks at

Ramadi, about thirty miles higher up the Euphrates. The operations culminated in General Brooking's brilliant victory at Ramadi on 27–28 September. A detachment of one hundred men accompanied General Brooking as his personal escort, but the remainder of the 14th Sikhs was left in garrison at Falluja and its neighbouring posts. During the period of concentration of Brooking's column, the 14th were constantly called upon for escorts and working parties. The Battalion received the personal thanks both of General Brooking and of the Chief Engineer of the 15th Division for the willing, cheerful and efficient manner in which these duties were carried out.

In October the 14th Sikhs were transferred from the 50th to the 51st Infantry Brigade–a new formation being organised in the Baghdad area as part of a new 17th Division, which also included the 34th and 52nd Infantry Brigades. The British force in Mesopotamia was being strengthened. The collapse of the. Russians had rendered our position less secure, especially as there were indications of a Turkish concentration in strength with the object of recapturing Baghdad.

Marching off from Falluja on 11 October, the 14th arrived four days later at Kadhimain, a suburb on the Tigris right bank a few miles north of Baghdad. There the Battalion joined the 1st Highland Light Infantry, 2nd Rajputs and 1/10th Gurkhas to form the 51st Brigade under Brigadier General R. J. T. Hildyard. Drafts amounting to over two hundred Indian ranks joined the Battalion from India before the end of the month.

At Kadhimain intensive battalion and brigade training was carried out for about six weeks. On 1 November the men of the 14th Sikhs distinguished themselves in a brigade sports meeting by winning nearly every event for which they entered. The weather during November was delightful.

On 8 December the 51st Brigade marched northwards from Kadhimain for Istabulat, a distance of about seventy miles. The march coincided with a spell of bitterly cold weather, and bivouacking in the open at night was far from enjoyable. The water in water-bottles froze solid at night. The 14th Sikhs were proud of being the only unit from which no man fell out during the entire march.

Istabulat was reached on 12 December. The remainder of the 51st Brigade halted there and went into standing camp but the 14th Sikhs (less two platoons left at Istabulat station) moved on to Samarra. There the Battalion was employed as guard over the aerodrome and store dumps, a task which entailed an extended piquet line and numerous duties. Hostile aeroplanes constantly dropped bombs, but with no effect.

1918

The 14th marched back to Istabulat towards the end of January 1918. [21] During the remainder of that month and throughout February much training was carried out. Gas masks were issued to our troops at this time, but they were never actually used in Mesopotamia. The Battalion was re-armed with high velocity rifles in February. Towards the end of the month a sepoy ran amuck, but was promptly and gallantly dealt with by Subadar Jiwan Singh, who was later awarded the Indian Distinguished Service Medal for "showing presence of mind and great personal bravery."

Early in March the 51st Brigade moved forward from Istabulat to Samarra, and during the latter part of the month the 17th Division was actively exercised in marches and manoeuvres between Samarra and Tikrit. The manoeuvres were undertaken mainly in the hope of mystifying the Turks higher up the Tigris and of diverting their attention from the operations of the 15th Division on the Euphrates which culminated in General Brooking's striking success at Khan Baghdadi. The exercises of the 17th Division thoroughly tested the marching powers and endurance of the men.

---

[21] On 1 January 1918 the following British officers were doing duty with the Battalion in Mesopotamia: Lieutenant Colonel E. S. Earle; Major M. Wace; Captains H. C. Finnis, R. A. Savory, G. F. Bunbury; Lieutenants W. J. Crocker, C. A. Maer, H. E. Winthrop, K. K. O'Connor; 2nd Lieutenant C. J. B. Church; Captain H. J. M. Cursetjee, I.M.S. (medical officer). Major G. Channer rejoined the battalion on 3 January.

The weather was stormy and there were numerous heavy thunderstorms. There were many long marches. In one of these the 14th Sikhs covered thirty-two miles without a single man falling out; next day they marched twenty-four miles. The Battalion was complimented several times by the brigade commander on the excellence of its marching. The 51st Brigade returned to Samarra on 31 March.

By this time it was clear that the Turks had given up all idea of attempting to recapture Baghdad. In April leave parties went off to India, and units settled down into camp and anticipated a quiet time during the approaching hot-weather season. Such anticipations were not entirely fulfilled.

In the first half of May I Corps advanced up the Tigris, with the object of holding the Turkish XVIII Corps at Fat-ha whilst the British III Corps operated against Kirkuk. Starting from Samarra on 4 May, I Corps reached Tikrit and remained in the vicinity of that town for about a week before withdrawing. There was no contact with the enemy and the only incident worth recording is an unpleasant march carried out on the night of 6 May by a column which included the 51st Brigade. This march started at 4 p.m. Torrential rain fell throughout the night, and it was intensely dark. The bulk of the column arrived at their destination at about 2:30 a.m.: but the field artillery and a large portion of the wheeled transport were compelled to halt at midnight and await daybreak before going farther. The rearguard eventually came in to camp at 9 a.m., having taken seventeen hours to cover eleven miles.

By 16 May the 14th Sikhs were back again in camp at Samarra. A few days later the 51st Brigade moved farther south to Istabulat.

Meanwhile, the critical situation in France had evoked an urgent call by the British Government on India for additional troops for overseas service. To help India, the Mesopotamia Force was called upon to provide a complete infantry company from each of sixty Indian infantry battalions. In this way fifteen battalions of trained men would be furnished, ready for immediate service elsewhere, while the sixty denuded battalions in Mesopotamia were filled up with recruits from India.

From the 14th Sikhs, A Company, under Major Wace, was detailed to go to India. The Company left battalion headquarters on 13 May. On arrival in India it was combined with companies drawn from the 36th Sikhs, 45th Sikhs and 52nd Sikhs to form a new battalion designated the 1/151st Infantry. To replace the gap in the 14th, a new A Company was formed by taking one platoon from each of the other three Companies, and then each Company formed its own fourth platoon. A draft of over one hundred men joined the Battalion early in June.

June 1918 was a hot month, but the camp at Istabulat was comfortable and all ranks were very happy there. Not for long, however, was comparative idleness to prevail. It was decided to extend the railway northwards from Samarra, and troops of I Corps were detailed to assist in the construction work. On 13 June a working party of the 14th Sikhs, four British officers and three hundred and ninety-five Indian ranks, under Major Channer, left Istabulat for this purpose. In the middle of July the headquarters of the Battalion were moved to Tikrit, whence a further hundred men were sent to join the detachment working on the railway.

The weather during July was hot, but the camps were free from sand flies and insect pests and the health of the Battalion continued to be good. Early in August the Battalion was concentrated at Tikrit, and thereafter throughout the month, which was comparatively cool, about four hundred men were supplied daily from headquarters for railway construction work. For two and a half months this work had considerably hampered purely military training; but in September – an exceptionally hot month – calls upon the 14th Sikhs for working parties were much-reduced.

In August an epidemic of influenza broke out in the British force in Mesopotamia and was very widespread. Fortunately the disease was not of such a serious type as in some other parts of the world, but for a time our fighting strength was seriously crippled. In the 14th Sikhs the total number of cases was two hundred and ninety-eight. At one period there were as many as one hundred and fifty men incapacitated at the same time. All cases were dealt with by the Battalion's medical establishment; none were evacuated to field ambulances and none proved fatal. As cases occurred, they were segregated in a part of the camp which gradually grew quite large. Captain Cursetjee and his medical staff did noble work, and Sub-Assistant Surgeon Bhagwan Singh deserves special mention for his untiring and able assistance to Captain Cursetjee. The epidemic died out before the middle of October.

In September it was generally understood in Mesopotamia that no more serious fighting in that region was to be anticipated. A number of officers were consequently granted short leave to England, and among them was Colonel Earle. Major Channer took over command of the 14th Sikhs. On 15 October Subadar Major Sham Singh Bahadur, I.D.S.M., left Mesopotamia for duty with the depot at Multan. He had done splendid service with the Battalion since it left India in October 1914. His place as Subadar Major was taken, by Subadar Narain Singh.[22]

---

[22] The British officers with the 14th Sikhs in Mesopotamia on 15 October 1918 were: Major G. Channer; Captains R. A. Savory, G. F. Bunbury and W. J. Crocker (Adjutant); Lieutenants H. V. Spankie, H. E. Winthrop (Quartermaster), K. K. O'Connor, C. J. B. Church and D. W. G. Humphreys: 2nd Lieutenant A. Irving; Captain H. J. M. Cursetjee, I.M.S. (Medical Officer).

CHAPTER 8

1918–1919

THE GREAT WAR: MESOPOTAMIA

We now come to the final phase of the Mesopotamia campaign: the British advance up the line of the Tigris on Mosul. This was carried out by General Cobbe with I Corps and two cavalry brigades, totalling in round numbers 2,800 sabres, 15,000 rifles and 130 guns. The hostile strength opposing him was considerably less.

The Turkish advanced position covering the approaches to Mosul lay astride the Fat-ha gorge, twenty-five miles north of Tikrit. It was of great natural strength. A second position, fifteen miles farther north about Mushak, was known also to have been prepared. The bulk of the Turkish strength was on the west bank of the Tigris and their line of communication back to Mosul lay on that bank. General Cobbe's plan of action aimed not merely at driving back the enemy, but at cutting him off from Mosul and destroying the major part of his force.

The British troops were organised into four groups - the 17th Division group, the 18th Division group (which included the 7th Cavalry Brigade), the 11th Cavalry Brigade and the Light Armoured Motor Brigade. We are here mainly concerned with the 17th Division, which included the 34th, 51st and 52nd Infantry Brigades. Each brigade at this time contained only three battalions, in addition to a machinegun company. Moreover, every Indian battalion included a number of very young soldiers, both officers and men; for not only had a complete company been withdrawn from every battalion during the summer, but numerous Officers and non-commissioned officers had been sent back also to form in India the nuclei of new battalions.

General Cobbe planned to strike his first blow on 24 October, when the 18th Division group on the east bank of the Tigris was to capture the Fat-ha east bank position. The 17th Division on the other side of the river was to demonstrate on a wide front against the Turkish west bank position but was not push home its attack until the 25th, that is, until the enemy's east bank position was in our hands. The 11th Cavalry Brigade, operating wide on the British right flank east of the Tigris, was on 24 October to reach a point on the Little Zab River well above its junction with the Tigris, and next day to work down the line of the Little Zab. The armoured car brigade was to operate wide on our left flank.

The 14th Sikhs under Major Channer, as part of the 51st Brigade of the 17th Division, started forward from Tikrit up the Tigris west bank on 20 October. By the evening of the 22nd the 52nd Brigade was established on a line within a mile of the enemy's trenches. After dark the 51st Brigade moved up and dug in on the right of the 52nd Brigade.

23 October, 1918

On the afternoon of the 23rd an infantry brigade of the 18th Division east of the river pushed forward so as to be in readiness to assault the Fat-ha east bank position next morning. On the west bank the 51st and 52nd Brigades advanced their line after dark for about half a mile, and the artillery of the 17th Division moved forward into positions to support the attack to be launched at dawn by the 18th Division. The 51st Brigade, with the Highland Light Infantry and 14th Sikhs in front line and 1/10th Gurkhas in support, was disposed on a narrow front in some depth with a view to the possibility of having to carry out an assault later. A few shots were fired during the night: the 14th Sikhs had one man slightly wounded.

24 October

The Turks did not wait for the assault of the 18th Division. Early in the night they abandoned their east bank position. On the west bank their piquets continued firing till 3:30 a.m., but by 5 a.m. on 24 October it was definitely ascertained that the enemy had abandoned his position there also. The H.L.I. and 14th Sikhs advanced at dawn and occupied the empty Turkish trenches on the steep hill to their front.

General Cobbe had hoped that successful action by the 18th Division east of the Tigris on the 24th would lead to a Turkish withdrawal during the ensuing night from the very strong west bank position. In the event, the enemy's retirement took place twenty-four hours earlier than had been anticipated.

Pursuit of the Turks was organised as speedily as possible. On the Tigris west bank the 52nd Brigade, preceded by a squadron of cavalry and two armoured cars, was to lead the way through the Fat-ha gorge. But the cavalry were much delayed in getting through; the armoured cars could not do so at all and the 52nd Brigade was held up. The narrow road curved tortuously round the foot of the hills near the river, crossing numerous ravines and dry watercourses. There were many hairpin bends and steep gradients, and in places the Turks had broken up the track by demolitions. Sappers and pioneers were hurried forward to execute repairs, but for some time the road was impracticable for wheeled transport.

The 51st Brigade had to take the lead in the advance of the 17th Division. The H.L.I. and 14th Sikhs, from the Turkish trenches that they had occupied, came down on the far side of the hill and then marched up the road. The third battalion of the brigade (the 10th Gurkhas), with a few mountain guns and machineguns, moved along the crest of the hill range on the west of the road as a left flank guard.

At 6 p.m. the two battalions on the road reached a point about seven miles above the Fat-ha gorge and there bivouacked for the night, covered by outposts provided by the H.L.I. The men were very tired. On the two previous nights they had scarcely slept at all, being busy digging trenches. They were to have only a few hours' sleep this night. It may be mentioned that the weather, though quite hot by day, was distinctly cold at night. As only a limited amount of transport was available for General Cobbe's operations, the troops were lightly equipped. The Sikhs carried one blanket apiece on the person; greatcoats had been left at Tikrit.

By nightfall on 24 October only the 51st Brigade of the 17th Division had advanced beyond the Fat-ha gorge. East of the Tigris the advanced troops of the 18th Division bivouacked about level with the 51st Brigade; on that bank, too the passage of the gorge had not been easy. Far away on the British right, General Cassels with his 11th Cavalry Brigade had carried out his allotted task and was in possession of a crossing over the Little Zab about twelve miles east of the junction of that river with the Tigris

25 October

Very early on 25 October the British advance was continued up both banks of the Tigris. The 17th Division had instructions to gain touch with the enemy and drive him back on to his Mushak position, assisted by the fire of the 18th Division heavy artillery from the east bank. The 18th Division, in addition to giving this assistance to the 77th Division, was to secure a crossing over the Little Zab.

On the west bank, the two battalions of the 51st Brigade on the road near the river began to move forward at 3 a.m., the Highlanders leading. The H.L.I. reached the vicinity of Qala Jabbar soon after 8 a.m., and there came under hostile shellfire. Brigadier General Hildyard, commanding the 51st Brigade, now received instructions not to get too closely engaged without sufficient support. The H.L.I., therefore, continued forward slowly and cautiously. Away on the left, the 10th Gurkhas advanced along the crest of the Jabal Makhul range, roughly level with the H.L.I. but separated from them by difficult hilly country.

By midday the H.L.I. were two miles north of Qala Jabbar in contact with the Turks in their Mushak position. The 14th Sikhs were held back some distance in rear. The headquarters of the 17th Division were at Qala Jabbar, where also by noon the 34th Brigade (less one battalion) and eight mountain guns had arrived. The 51st Brigade made no further advance before dark.

The 52nd Brigade was still south of the Fat-ha gorge, immobilised by lack of transport. It had been found that carts on the road completely blocked all traffic in the opposite direction and it had therefore been decided to use pack transport only. To effect this, all transport mules had to be withdrawn from the 52nd to meet the needs of the 51st and 34th Brigades.

In the afternoon, misled by an inaccurate report, General Cobbe ordered the 17th Division to press its attack vigorously and the 18th Division to support the 17th by advancing up the east bank of the Tigris beyond its junction with the Little Zab. The 18th Division could not advance beyond the Little Zab, for its leading infantry brigade was unable to complete the passage of that river before dusk. One of its field batteries went into action near the Little Zab-Tigris junction, but there came under accurate hostile shellfire and suffered heavily.

General Cobbe's order to the 17th Division did not reach its commander till 5 p.m.; and darkness had fallen before the H.L.I, at the head of the 51st Brigade, moved forward. Apparently they were told that little, if any, opposition was to be expected, for it was thought at Corps headquarters that the Turks had already begun to evacuate their Mushak position. At about 8 p.m. the Highlanders came up against a strong Turkish piquet posted astride and to the west of the road. They assaulted and captured the post, but their losses in doing this and then consolidating their position amounted to over one hundred. Two companies of the 14th Sikhs were sent forward to support the H.L.I., but were withdrawn at 10 p.m. There was only one Sikh casualty. The 14th bivouacked for the night in a nullah near the road, close to 51st Brigade headquarters and over a mile in rear of the position of the H.L.I.

By midnight the British advanced troops were disposed as follows:

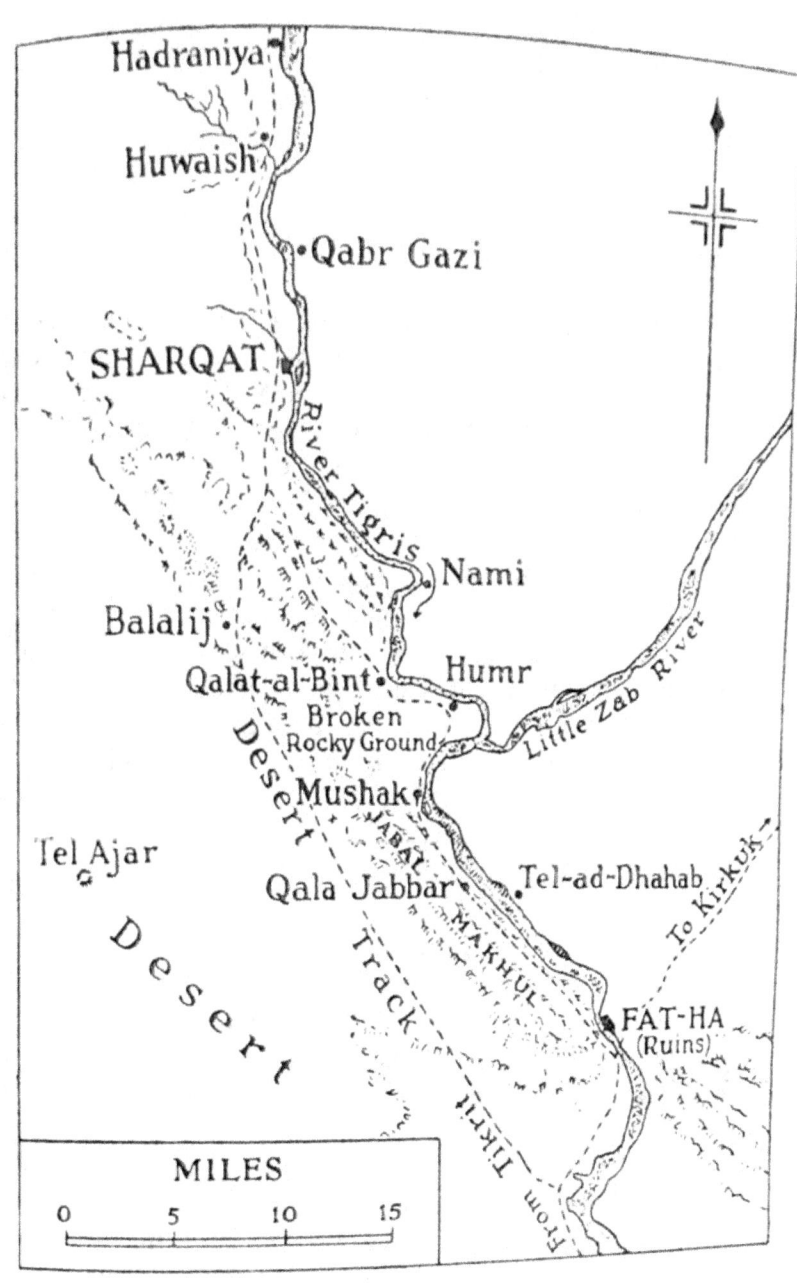

MESOPOTAMIA. THE RIVER TIGRIS.
October, 1918.

East of the Tigris, three groups were established on the northern bank of the Little Zab River – Cassels' cavalry brigade being twelve miles, the 7th Cavalry Brigade five miles, and one infantry brigade and field battery of the 18th Division two miles eastward of the Little Zab-Tigris junction. The remainder of the 18th Division were strung out to the south of the Little Zab, which a bridging train had reached after dark.

West of the Tigris, the H.LI., in close contact with the enemy, held a position astride the road, and in broken foothills to the west of it, about a mile south of Mushak. To the left, on the crest of the Jabal Makhul one and a half miles south-west of the H.L.I. was Colonel Coningham's column of the 1/10th Gurkhas, four mountain guns and two machinegun sections. The 51st Brigade headquarters, with the 14th Sikhs, two machinegun sections and eight mountain guns, were one and a half miles in rear of the H.L.I. At Qala Jabbar, two miles farther back along the road, were the 17th Division headquarters with the 34th Infantry Brigade (less one battalion) and two field howitzer batteries. These batteries had been brought forward thus far only with the greatest difficulty. During the night one of them, the 403rd Battery, joined 51st Brigade headquarters. Farther back, two more field batteries had succeeded after great efforts in getting through the Fat-ha gorge, but were still five miles short of Qala Jabbar.

The orders issued by General Cobbe after dark on 25 October for operations next day were based on the erroneous supposition that the Turks intended to retire from their Mushak position during the night. The 11th Cavalry Brigade (Cassels) was to move early, ford the Tigris thirteen miles north of Shargat and intercept the enemy's retreat. A group consisting of the 7th Cavalry Brigade and troops of other arms from the 18th Division was to advance before daylight along the Tigris east bank direct on Sharqat. (The orders for this group were modified later.) The 17th Division was to continue to gain ground during the night and to pursue along the west bank.

The enemy's position facing the advanced troops of the 17th Division lay just south of a point where the Tigris bends in westward almost to the edge of the road. West of the road the Turkish defences, facing south, were skilfully sited along the broken rugged hills; from the road for several hundred yards eastward towards the Tigris bank the enemy had dug a line of trenches, covered by wire entanglement, along flat ground. Subsequent inspection showed that the Turkish left, or eastern, flank had been made especially strong. The western portion of the Tigris bed was dry and, to protect themselves against a possible British advance along the river bank and bed, the Turks had constructed on the hill slopes west of the road behind their front line a series of trenches and machinegun emplacements facing eastward.

From the point where the British 51st Brigade headquarters were located the lines of approach to the enemy's position were of entirely different character on either side of the road. West of the road there was a tangled mass of broken, steep and precipitous hills: the road ran closely under the hill-sides: to the east between the road and the river was a low lying strip of flat ground. If it had been realised that the enemy intended to hold on to his Mushak position on 26 October, no doubt the British tactics would have been different. As, however, it was thought that the Turks would only offer a weak rearguard resistance, the speediest method of a direct attack across the flat ground east of the road was decided upon.

26 October

Before dawn on 26 October several reports from the H.LI. stated that the enemy was still holding his trenches in strength. Nevertheless General Hildyard, in view of the instructions given him, decided not to alter his plan of attack. The 14th Sikhs were to advance over the flat ground east of the road, and, when they came up level with the H.L.I., the two battalions were to continue forward together.

At daybreak the two foremost companies of the H.L.I. on their own initiative attempted to advance, but were quickly forced back. About the same time the 14th Sikhs, some two thousand yards in rear of the H.L.I., began to deploy into artillery formation on a frontage of five hundred yards with their left on the road. A Company on the left, and C Company were in front line; B and D Companies in support. Four of the Battalion Lewis guns, under 2nd Lieutenant Irving, had already been sent to work along the hills on the west of the road to assist the advance from that flank. A section of the 51st Brigade machinegun company accompanied the Battalion on its right rear. The advance was to be supported by the fire of eight mountain guns in position on the hill slopes west of the road and of the 403rd Howitzer Battery in position to the east of the road.

Their deployment completed, the 14th began to advance at 6.25 a.m. Almost immediately the Battalion came under artillery fire, and casualties began to occur. The advance was continued steadily. Platoons gradually opened out into half-platoons in fours or file, subsequently extending as they came under machine gun, or rifle, fire. The ground traversed was mostly covered with thick thorn and scrub, three to five feet high, and this rendered control and communication somewhat difficult. The hostile artillery fire, though galling, did not cause undue casualties. It was not long however before the battalion began to suffer heavily from intense machinegun fire. This fire, mainly delivered from the hills to the left front, was accurate and deadly. The men continued to push forward very gallantly, in spite of severe casualties. Three of the four company commanders were wounded and put out of action quite early.

By about 7:30 a.m. the Battalion front line, which had previously been reinforced by D Company from support, had almost reached the enemy's wire. But the attack was now definitely checked. A Company, on the left, joined up with the H.L.I. on the foothills just west of the road. The other two companies in front line fell back a short distance upon the company in support; and all three companies took up a line and reformed in a shallow depression about three hundred yards from the enemy's wire: there they stayed for the remainder of the day.

The attack of the 14th Sikhs had been supported by gunfire. The mountain artillery shells, however, were quite ineffective against the well-entrenched enemy, while the fire of the howitzers was more than neutralised by hostile gunfire. With all the advantage of command and of concealed positions in the hills, the Turkish guns quickly put the 403rd Battery out of action and inflicted severe casualties upon the personnel.

It was quite clear by 8 a.m. that the enemy was holding his position in strength. Further progress by the H.L.I. and 14th Sikhs was out of the question: both battalions were held up in close contact with the enemy, and both battalions had suffered severe casualties. Away on the left, the 10th Gurkhas on the crest of the Jabal Makhul were also meeting with considerable opposition on difficult ground.

Meanwhile, Brigadier General Wauchope, with two battalions of his 34th Brigade had reached General Hildyard's headquarters. Thinking that there was danger of a Turkish counterattack against the right of the 51st Brigade, Wauchope sent two companies of 114th Mahrattas to secure that flank. The Mahrattas, advancing to the east of the line taken by the 14th Sikhs, finally reached a dry island in the Tigris bed and there remained for the rest of the day, well away to the right front of the 14th. They suffered nearly one hundred casualties from artillery and machine gun fire.

At 10 a.m. the 404th Howitzer Battery reached the front and came into action near the 403rd Battery. Half an hour later Wauchope sent the 112th Infantry up into the hills to secure the left of the H.L.I. and gain connection with the 10th Gurkhas. This the 112th effected successfully with the loss of only one casualty. About midday General Leslie, commander of the 17th Division came forward to the headquarters of the H.L.I. to see the situation there personally. He decided to refrain from attempting any further advance that day.

At nightfall the advanced infantry line was moved back somewhat and reorganised. The 14th Sikhs were withdrawn and placed in reserve behind the H.L.I. The third battalion of the 34th Brigade (2nd Queen's Own Royal West Kent), which reached the front at dusk, was also held in reserve.

Casualties in the 14th Sikhs on 26 October totalled 323, or about 38 percent of the strength engaged. Most of the casualties were caused by machinegun fire, and nearly all were incurred between 6:30 and 7:30 a.m. The Battalion went into action with 8 British officers, 15 Indian officers and 832 other ranks. Of the British officers, 2nd Lieutenant Irving was killed; Major Channer (who remained at duty), Captain Bunbury, Lieutenants O'Connor, Church and Humphreys were wounded. One Indian officer was killed and four were wounded. Of the other ranks 65 were killed and 247 wounded. On the evening of the 26th Captain Savory, who had been attached to the brigade staff for the past three days, rejoined the Battalion.

The labours of the medical establishment deserve special mention. At the regimental aid post Captain Cursetjee and Sub-Assistant Surgeon Bhagwan Singh were at work almost continuously from the night of the 25th to the late evening of 27 October. The Battalion stretcher bearers were busy most of the night of the 25th in assisting to evacuate casualties of the H.L.I. All day on the 26th and 27th they were dealing with casualties of the 14th Sikhs. Almost all the Battalion casualties were evacuated by its own stretcher bearers, a large proportion being stretcher cases. The stretcher bearers were constantly under fire on the 26th, but fortunately only suffered one casualty. On the 27th, when the Battalion advanced the medical establishment was only able to keep touch with headquarters by handing over all casualties to the quartermaster (Lieutenant Winthrop), who had brought up food and blankets for them. No field ambulance had as yet come up.

During 26 October General Cassels with his 11th Cavalry Brigade successfully carried out his mission. After crossing the river by a difficult ford at Hadraniya, fifteen miles north of Sharqat, he moved southward for a few miles down the west bank of the Tigris and by nightfall had occupied a favourable position at Huwaish astride the Sharqat-Mosul road, thus blocking the Turkish line of retreat.

By the evening of the 26th it was believed at General Cobbe's headquarters that strong Turkish reinforcements had reached Sharqat and that this was the cause of the unexpected resistance of the enemy at Mushak. For the morrow's operations General Cobbe instructed the 17th Division to attack vigorously, its main pressure being directed along the crest of the Jabal Makhul, and the 18th Division to assist the 17th by gunfire across the Tigris. He also gave orders for the 7th Cavalry Brigade and one infantry brigade of the 18th Division to cross from the east to the west bank of the river, by a bridge which had been reconstructed at Fat-ha, and form a corps reserve.

At nightfall on 25 October, British headquarters had been most confident that the Turks would retire from the Mushak position that night; but anticipations were not fulfilled. At nightfall on the 26th it was believed that the enemy intended to hold on to the Mushak position next day. Again anticipations proved incorrect, for during the night the Turks withdrew.

27 October

In the early morning of 27 October patrols of the 51st Brigade found that the Turks had retired all along their line. As soon as it was clear to him that the enemy was in full retreat, General Cobbe cancelled his orders of the previous evening and directed the 18th Division to push troops at once up the Tigris east bank, both to prevent the Turks crossing to that side of the river and to support General Cassels. Meantime, the commander of the 12th Division instructed General Wauchope to advance at once in pursuit with his 34th Infantry Brigade and certain other troops. The 51st Brigade was to have a short rest before following in support.

Wauchope's progress was somewhat slow. He was hampered by the initial deployment of his infantry, the dispersion of his units, the bad road and the difficult, hilly country. However, the bulk of his troops reached Qalat-al-Bint and went into bivouac there at about 6 p.m. Of the 51st Brigade, the H.L.I. and 14th Sikhs started forward at 3 p.m. and three hours later halted near Humr. On the left flank, Colonel Coningham's column (now reinforced by the 45th Sikhs from the 52nd Brigade) advanced along the crest of the Jabal Makhul and bivouacked for the night at Balalij.

East of the Tigris, General Sanders, marching northwards with a brigade group of the 18th Division, reached a point east of Sharqat at 8 p.m. There he left one battalion to piquet the river and continued his march northwards.

During the day the 11th Cavalry Brigade maintained its position at Huwaish astride the Turkish line of retreat. The situation, however, was not too comfortable, for towards the end of the day the approach of Turkish reinforcements from the north began to threaten Cassels' rear.

To General Cobbe it seemed probable that the Turks, leaving a small rearguard to delay and hold off the 17th Division, would with greatly superior strength attempt to break through the 11th Cavalry Brigade. General Cobbe could not know, of course, that Cassels had skilfully succeeded in creating an exaggerated impression of his strength in the mind of the Turkish commander. The distance between Cassels at Huwaish and the advanced troops of the 17th Division at Qalat-al-Bint and Balalij was quite twenty-five miles; and the intervening area was difficult, rough and hilly – ideal ground for rearguard delaying tactics. The danger threatening Cassels led Cobbe to press the 17th Division to continue its advance with the utmost speed, regardless of exhaustion. His orders at nightfall on the 27th were for the division to continue the pursuit during the night, to gain contact and to attack the enemy vigorously as early as possible in the morning. East of the Tigris, Sanders group was to push on to Cassels' support and the 7th Cavalry Brigade from Fat-ha was to move with the utmost speed to reinforce him.

28 October

On 28 October, Cassels at Huwaish was attacked from the south, as had been anticipated. Fortunately, the Turks did not develop their full strength against him and he was able to hold his own without much difficulty. At the same time, some of his cavalry delayed the approach of the enemy from the north, retiring slowly before their advance.

East of the Tigris, Sanders, after marching all night, came into touch with Cassels very early on the 28th. Besides assisting him during the day by gunfire across the river, Sanders reinforced Cassels by one battalion sent across the Tigris by a ferry which had been established two miles north of Hadraniya. The 7th Cavalry Brigade, after marching about forty-five miles from Fat-ha, reached the Hadraniya ford at 4 p.m. and began to cross the Tigris. It then proceeded to guard Cassels' rear against the Turkish reinforcements approaching from the north.

Meanwhile, west of the Tigris, the advance of the 17th Division had begun at 3 a.m., when Wauchope's group marched off from Qalat-al-Bint and Hildyard with his two battalions of the 51st Brigade started from the vicinity of Humr. Progress in the dark was slow. The heights on either side of the route had to be searched for hostile parties, and the road itself was rough and intersected by a number of deep ravines which were serious obstacles to the passage of the artillery. Touch was gained with enemy at 8 a.m. At this hour General Leslie, commander of the 17th Division, joined Wauchope and took over general control at the front.

The Turkish rearguard was holding a position about eleven miles from Qalat-al-Bint, near the point where the road leading down from Balalij joined the route from Humr to Sharqat. Wauchope attacked the enemy between 12:30 and 2 p.m. and was entirely successful, the Turks leaving about two hundred prisoners and several machineguns in our hands.

The 51st Brigade caught up with Wauchope about the time the attack on the Turkish rearguard had come to a successful conclusion. Colonel Coningham's column from Balalij also joined in during the afternoon.

The Turks made a rapid retreat, and Wauchope's advanced patrols lost touch with the enemy. Moreover, owing to the heat of the day, the shortage of water and their recent exertions, all the advanced troops of the 17th Division now collected under General Leslie were by this time greatly exhausted. The animals were dead beat. Leslie decided, therefore, not to advance any farther that day, and the 17th Division bivouacked three miles south of Sharqat. The 14th Sikhs provided outposts.

29 October

At 1:45 a.m. on 29 October the 51st Brigade, three machinegun sections and twelve mountain guns moved forward again as advanced guard. The 14th Sikhs, on outpost duty, closed and marched in the rear. The 34th Brigade did not start from bivouac till 6 a.m., half an hour before sunrise.

Progress during the hours of darkness was very slow. The ground was much broken, and in the dim moonlight great difficulty was experienced in keeping to the ill-defined track. North of Sharqat the ground between the road and the Tigris was flat and low lying. The road itself ran below the eastern edge of a rough plateau which rose abruptly to the west. Across this plateau the Turkish rearguard had retired. Contact with it was gained at about 7 a.m., three miles north of Sharqat.

The 51st Brigade now advanced against the enemy on a broad front to the west of the road, with the H.L.I. and 10th Gurkhas in the front line. Making skilful use of the natural advantages of the ground for delaying action, the Turkish rearguard fell back slowly. At about 9 a.m. the 14th Sikhs were moved up in Support of the Gurkhas on the left, with instructions to keep one thousand yards in rear of them. The 45th Sikhs (attached to the 51st Brigade) were held back as brigade reserve. A field battery and a mountain gun battery had come into action to support the advancing infantry.

The British advance continued steadily, if slowly at 11 a.m. General Leslie learned from an air report that the Turks were holding a position on the plateau about three miles south of Huwaish. The general line ran westward from the road for two miles and then bent back to the north-west. The position had evidently been hastily prepared and its trenches were not continuous, but were arranged in depth in numerous short lengths.

By midday the H.L.I. and 10th Gurkhas had reached a line about fourteen hundred yards south of the Turkish position. They were on a wide frontage of about two miles, and in their advance over the broken plateau had become somewhat scattered. The right of the Highlanders rested on the eastern edge of the plateau. There was a gap between them and the Gurkhas. Further advance on this broad front against the enemy in position was not a practical proposition without reinforcement and closer artillery support. At this hour the 14th Sikhs were about half a mile in rear of the Gurkha centre, the 45th near the road over a mile to the right rear of the H.L.I., and the 34th Brigade on the road half a mile in rear of the 45th Sikhs.

General Leslie had not more than three thousand rifles and thirty-four guns at his immediate disposal. The strength of the Turks holding the trenches in front of him was uncertain. (It was actually about four thousand infantry and six batteries of artillery.) Leslie decided to deliver an assault, with the 45th Sikhs and the 34th Brigade, against the enemy's left front on a frontage of eight hundred yards. There were difficulties in the way of ensuring close artillery support. Gun ammunition was rather short, due to the difficulty of transport over the forty miles from Fat-ha; accurate observation of the enemy's irregular and ill-defined position by forward observing officers was not easy; and no aeroplane was available for observation work. Zero hour was finally fixed at 4 p.m.

At that hour the assaulting column, headed by the 45th Sikhs, started its advance from a point about a mile south of the line occupied by the H.L.I.; there was much dust and visibility was bad. The 45th Sikhs, after passing through the H.L.I., swung to their left and pushed on to within six hundred yards of the enemy's trenches. The Turks, however, launched a following strong counterattack. The 45th, with half the 114th Mahrattas in close support, were forced back; but the enemy's effort was then checked. Confused fighting went on till well after dark. The British assault had failed, though on the left flank the 112th Infantry (of the 34th Brigade) actually captured some Turkish trenches just as it was getting dark.

Part of the Turkish counterattack which drove back the head of the British assaulting column at about 5 p.m. struck against the extended line of the 10th Gurkhas. This line had been reinforced earlier in the afternoon by two companies of the 14th Sikhs under Captain Savory, and the remainder of the 14th were close at hand near the Gurkha battalion headquarters. The enemy here was repulsed without much difficulty.

General Leslie's front line at nightfall lay at an angle to the enemy's position. On the left the 112th Infantry were at close grips with the Turks. The 114th Mahrattas were to the right rear of the 112th. The 45th Sikhs were between the 114th and the H.L.I. After dark the 14th Sikhs were moved to their right to relieve the 45th, who went back into reserve. The 2nd Royal West Kent Regiment (34th Brigade) and 10th Gurkhas formed supports in rear of the 114th Mahrattas and 112th Infantry respectively.

In the meantime, General Cassels at Huwaish had been undisturbed by the Turks on his southern and western fronts, and during the day his position was strengthened considerably by the arrival of some infantry and artillery of the 18th Division from the east bank of the Tigris. On his northern front the 7th Cavalry Brigade fought a brilliantly successful action against the Turkish reinforcements which were moving southward.

During the night of 29 October the men of the 17th Division, unaware of the hopeless position of the enemy, fully expected battle to be renewed at daybreak. It was therefore a welcome surprise when at daybreak on the 30th white flags were seen to be flying all along the enemy's front. The Turkish forces surrendered and the enemy's army in Mesopotamia practically ceased to exist.

With the further advance of part of the British forces to Mosul we are not here concerned. An armistice with the Turks came into force on 31 October, and the Mesopotamia campaign came to an end.

The casualties of the 17th Division on 29 October amounted to about five hundred out of the three thousand riflemen General Leslie had in action that day. The 45th Sikhs and 114th Mahrattas were the chief sufferers, with losses of 186 and 163 respectively. The casualties of the other infantry battalions were: 10th Gurkhas, 64; 112th Infantry, 46; 14th Sikhs, 27; and Highland Light Infantry, 23.

Between 18 and 30 October 1918, General Cobbe's force captured 11,322 prisoners, fifty-one guns and much war material. The total British casualties during the same period were 1,886, of which 1,504 were incurred by the 17th Division. In that division the highest casualties were suffered by the following:

14th Sikhs	352
114th Mahrattas	291
1st Highland Light Infantry	256
45th Sikhs	187
2nd Royal West Kent	119
1/10th Gurkhas	107
112th Infantry	47

The casualties of Cassels' 11th Cavalry Brigade totalled 181 men, of which the 7th Hussars incurred 86. The 7th Cavalry Brigade lost 63 men in all. The losses of the 18th Division were very slight.

The greatest strain during the last ten days' fighting of the Mesopotamian campaign fell undoubtedly on the advanced troops of the 17th Division. In this period only one man of the 14th Sikhs became a sick casualty or fell out of the ranks on the march – a havildar, who was taken ill on 25 October and died of pneumonia three days later; undoubtedly a belated case of influenza. A word of praise is due to the Battalion quartermaster and transport officer, Lieutenant H. E. Winthrope for the admirable manner in which he carried out his duties in most difficult circumstances; his arrangements for bringing forward food and water worked well and never failed.

The following of the 14th Sikhs were awarded "immediate" honours for the period of the final operations :

Major G. Channer   Distinguished Service Order.

Captain H. J. M. Cursetjee, I.M.S. Lieutenant H. V. Spankie Lieutenant K. K. O'Connor Subadar Narain Singh, I.D.S.M. Subadar Jaimal Singh Sub-Assistant Surgeon Jemadar Bhagwan Singh	Military Cross.
Jemadar Partab Singh Jemadar Mewa Singh	Indian Order of Merit, 2nd Class.
Jemadar Diwan Singh eight other ranks:	Indian Distinguished Service Medal.

The end of the Mesopotamian campaign, followed almost immediately by the armistice with Germany, did not involve an early return of the 14th Sikhs to India. The Battalion remained in Mesopotamia for another seven months.

1919

The Battalion was stationed north of Baghdad until the end of January 1919, when it moved to Basra. A farewell message from General Leslie, commander of the 17th Division, ran:

> On your departure from the 17th Division, Major General Leslie wishes all Officers and Ranks good-bye and continued success wherever you go. Your conduct, discipline and soldierly qualities while in the Division have been excellent, and you have done whatever you have undertaken, whether at play, at work or in battle, in a manner worthy of your high reputation and traditions. By parting with you the Division loses one of its finest regiments and does so with the greatest regret.

At Basra the Battalion was quartered in lines constructed on the site of an old graveyard and surrounded by inundated palm groves, an unhealthy and feverish spot. Guard duties were very heavy. All ranks were anticipating an early return to India, but the Battalion did not actually sail from Basra until 23 May 1919. Its embarkation strength was 5 British officers, 22 Indian officers and 772 other ranks. Lieutenant Colonel E. S. Earle, who had returned early in March from leave in England, was in command.

CHAPTER 9

1919–1933, INDIA

THE 1st BATTALION, 11th SIKH REGIMENT

After four and a half years of overseas service, the 14th Sikhs arrived back in India on 28 May 1919. They disembarked at Karachi, where they were most hospitably entertained by the local "welcome committee." On 31 May the Battalion left Karachi by train without knowledge of its destination. An immediate move to the Frontier was not anticipated, for Colonel Earle had with him only four British officers, no Lewis guns and no ammunition at all. However, the destination turned out to be Tank, on the Waziristan frontier.

WAZIRISTAN BORDER, June-September 1919

The Third Afghan War was in progress, and there was a general tribal uprising in Waziristan. A considerable number of troops had to be sent to the Waziristan frontier, and at one time a Mahsud attack in strength on Tank city had been feared. Soon after the 14th Sikhs reached Tank, however, the general situation improved.

Before long, the Battalion was split up into four portions. Headquarters with C Company remained at Tank; the other three companies garrisoned posts to the westward: B Company went to

Jandola, D Company to Khirgi and A Company to Murtaza. The last named was our outpost in the Gomal.

In June the garrisons of the various British posts were but little harassed by the tribesmen, but previously there had been much raiding of convoys. Most of the convoy escorts were found from post garrisons, one escort handing over to the next on the route between posts, and constant vigilance was necessary. Tank city and certain vulnerable and attractive portions of Tank cantonment such as the supply depot and the camel lines were objects of almost nightly raids by the enemy. Hence C and headquarters, in common with the remainder of the Tank garrison, were heavily pressed for duties on the perimeter and Tank city.

The health of the 14th Sikhs was far from satisfactory. The men were saturated with malaria. This was undoubtedly due in great measure to the conditions in Basra between January and May.
Moreover, the hot weather of 1919 was exceptionally severe and trying in the Tank district.

Two senior Indian officers of the Regiment died of heatstroke in June. Towards the end of that month cholera broke out in labour units at Tank. The epidemic spread fast, and it was some time before the medical officers were able to trace its origin and check its further development. Fortunately, no cholera cases occurred in the 14th.

By 18 August the companies in the outposts had been relieved by other troops, and the whole Battalion was concentrated at Tank. No fighting had taken place at the outposts beyond a little occasional sniping by the enemy, but duties had always been heavy. No incident of importance relieved the monotony of daily routine at Tank between the middle of August and the end of September. On 29 September the Battalion left Tank by rail and arrived at Multan next day.

MULTAN, October 1919-September 1920

The 14th Sikhs spent a year in Multan; a year of demobilisation and reorganisation. It was a trying period for the British officers and for all ranks, as indeed it was for the bulk of the Indian Army. The Afghan War was over; but operations on a large scale were necessary in Waziristan, where many Indian units were employed. No British infantry were available for this service, for the regular battalions which had recently arrived from England to replace the Territorials were for the time being merely collections of inexperienced recruits. For a year or so the Indian Army had to 'hold the fort' in India, and it is greatly to the credit of the Indian Army that matters proceeded as smoothly as they did.

After the return of the Regiment to Multan many men wished to take their discharge. They were legally entitled to be discharged if they so desired, but at the same time it had been decreed that Indian battalions must not fall below a certain strength. The glamour and inducements of military service were temporarily in abeyance, and very few recruits were obtainable. The result was that demobilisation had to proceed very gradually. It was thought that many of the men wishing to be discharged would change their minds after a spell of leave in their homes, and in some measure this forecast was correct. As many men as possible were granted leave: but at the end of the leave period there still remained far more men desirous of discharge than could be allowed to go. However they accepted the situation philosophically and with good spirit.

The Depot of the 14th Sikhs was absorbed into the Battalion on its arrival at Multan. The work at the Depot throughout the War, from 1914 to 1919, had been most arduous and exacting – the successive commandants, Majors Field and Daniell, had carried out their task with great success. In one respect they were notably successful, for at the end of the War the Depot of the Regiment was one of the few Indian depots whose accounts were in good order and not in hopeless confusion!

Lieutenant Colonel Earle left the Regiment on leave pending retirement in November 1919, handing over the command to Major

Channer. In January 1920, Lieutenant Colonel Talbot returned to duty with the Battalion after an absence of nearly six years and commanded it until he was transferred to a staff appointment in May the same year. Major Channer then resumed command.

In spite of the many difficulties, the reorganisation of the Battalion was practically complete by the end of September. The state of efficiency was as yet by no means up to pre-War standard, and it came as a surprise when orders were received to move from Multan to the Khyber Pass, i.e. once again to more or less active service conditions. It was not realised that actually the Regiment was far more efficient than the majority of Indian units at that time.

KHYBER, October 1920-November 1921

The 14th Sikhs left Multan by train on 1 October and arrived at Jamrud next day. There they remained for a fortnight, during which period Major Channer went on leave pending retirement, and Captain Savory took over command. On 15 October the Battalion marched up the Khyber Pass to Ali Masjid, where it remained encamped until November 1921.

Its camp was on a ridge above and to the crest of Ali Masjid village. The ridge was guarded at night by a series of piquets round a barbed-wire perimeter in which were enclosed the lines of the 14th and those of the hospital, a mountain battery and a section of a machinegun company. Below in the trough of the Khyber gorge, lay the lower camp containing a supply depot, transport lines, rest camp and some other small units. Guards and duties were heavy. In addition to piquets on the upper camp perimeter, the Battalion occupied (with strengths varying from one section to two platoons) seven posts in the Pass. Two of these were located about six miles away from battalion headquarters on the road towards Landi Kotal.

Early in January 1921, Major Daniell returned from sick leave in England and took over command of the Battalion, but he left again two months later on retirement. Captain Savory then officiated in command until Lieutenant Colonel C. F. W. Hughes, from the 15th Sikhs, took over in April 1921. Colonel Hughes remained with the

Battalion for seven months only, and in November Lieutenant Colonel J. G. Cadell (from the 45th Sikhs) was appointed commandant.

JULLUNDUR, 1921–1922

Early in November 1921 the 14th Sikhs were moved from the Khyber to Jullundur, as a temporary measure, and the bulk of the Regiment was sent on long leave prior to the despatch of the Battalion on duty overseas to Iraq– the country hitherto known as Mesopotamia. The men returned from leave to battalion headquarters at Jullundur early in February 1922. Unfortunately, during their leave of absence, a few of the younger soldiers had become imbued with the subversive *Akali* doctrines which at that time political agitators in the Punjab were doing their utmost to stimulate in order to undermine the loyalty of Sikh troops. There was a certain amount of insubordination, and eight men had to be dealt with by court-martial.

IRAQ, February 1922-January 1924

The Battalion left Jullundur on 20 February 1922 for Iraq. On arrival in that country it went to Hinaidi, on the outskirts of Baghdad, for garrison duty. Later in the year it moved to Kutal Amara, where it was employed in closing down the military cantonment and demolishing the post.

Early in 1922, Colonel Cadell was invalided to England. He did not return to the East, although he remained nominal commandant of the Battalion until April 1924.

The 11th SIKH REGIMENT

An important change in the organisation of Indian infantry was inaugurated in 1922. Single battalion regiments were abolished and battalions were grouped into regiments bearing new titles. The 14th Sikhs lost their identity as such, and became the 1st Battalion (King George's Own) (Ferozepore Sikhs) of the 11th Sikh Regiment. Under the new system a regiment was to comprise 'active' battalions and one 'training' battalion, which was to be located permanently at its station, would train recruits for the whole regiment, and in time of war act as the regimental depot.

The 11th Sikh Regiment was formed as follows

The 14th Sikhs became	1st Battalion 11th Sikh Regiment
The 15th Sikhs became	2nd Battalion 11th Sikh Regiment
The 45th Sikhs became	3rd Battalion 11th Sikh Regiment
The 36th Sikhs became	4th Battalion 11th Sikh Regiment
The 47th Sikhs became	5th Battalion 11th Sikh Regiment
The 35th Sikhs became	10th Training Battalion 11th Sikh Regiment

Nowshera was fixed upon as the permanent location of the Training Battalion. As for class composition, the 1st, 2nd and 3rd Battalions were to consist entirely of Sikhs, while the 4th and 5th comprised half Sikhs and half Punjabi Mohammedans. Active battalions were organised into four rifle companies and one headquarters company.

To return to Iraq. Early in 1923 the old 14th Sikhs were back again at Baghdad in the vicinity of the Royal Air Force aerodrome, the protection of which was their main role.

At this time, tribesmen in Kurdistan under the leadership of Shaikh Mahmud were actively hostile to the British administration. They had met with some success in the autumn of 1922, but the winter weather held operations in check, and it was not until the spring of 1923 that Shaikh Mahmud was finally dealt with.

Prior to this, A and B Companies of the 1/11th Sikhs, under Captains Maclaren and Spankie, left Baghdad by train on

20 February for Kingarban en route to Kirkuk. To cover the distance between Kingarban and Kirkuk would entail a week's marching. But troops were at the moment urgently required at Kirkuk, and the two companies were therefore transported thither by air on 21 February. This was the first occasion in history on which any considerable body of troops was thus carried by air to meet a military crisis. The two companies, in full fighting equipment, were moved in nine troop carrying aeroplanes, and the actual journey in the air took less than one hour.

KURDISTAN OPERATIONS, May-June 1923

The punitive operations against Shaikh Mahmud and his following were carried out in May and June. Our troops in this expedition acted under the supreme direction of the commander of the Royal Air Force in Iraq, and air forces for the operations were based on Mosul, Kirkuk and Arbil. For work on the ground the troops were divided into two columns. Of these, that which was formed at Kirkuk under Colonel-Commandant B. Vincent was termed Koicol and consisted of the 1/11th Sikhs (under Major H. F. Story), the 1/13th Frontier Force Rifles, the 3/16th Punjab Regiment, one pack battery and a company of Sappers and Miners.

The column marched off from Kirkuk 12 May. For a fortnight the troops traversed the Kurdistan country making many long marches; but there was little actual fighting, and no casualties were suffered. By 28 May the column was concentrated near Sulaimania, where it remained until 18 June when the troops marched back to Kirkuk and the column dispersed. The 1/11th Sikhs remained at Kirkuk until the end of September and then moved to Baghdad. For their services in Kurdistan Major Story received brevet promotion to Lieutenant Colonel and Subadar Bogh Singh was awarded the Military Cross.

SANTA CRUZ, 1924

In January 1924 the Battalion returned to India and was stationed for the next year at Santa Cruz, near Bombay. After Colonel Cadell's retirement in April 1924, Lieutenant Colonel B. H. Finnis was appointed to the Battalion as commandant, but he never actually joined, and during the period at Santa Cruz Major F. G. Swayne officiated in command. He became commandant on 1 February 1925.

MHOW, 1925–1927

The 1/11th Sikhs moved in February 1925 from Santa Cruz to Mhow, where they were stationed until November 1927. In 1926 the Battalion was the winner in the Punjab Native Army Hockey Tournament, for the first time since 1908. Lieutenant Colonel H. F. Story became commandant in October 1927.

WAZIRISTAN, 1928–1929

In the following month the Battalion left Mhow for Waziristan. Permission was obtained to break journey at Ferozepore, where a most successful battalion reunion was held. This took place from 8 to 12 November 1927, and was attended by fifty pensioned Indian officers and four hundred and fifty pensioned Indian other ranks. In Waziristan the Battalion was stationed for the first year at Damdil and for the second at Razmak. It left Waziristan for Nowshera in October 1929.

Colonel Story had given up command of the 1/11th Sikhs in April. Major R. F. Francis, M.C., then officiated as commandant for three months before handing over to Lieutenant Colonel L. M. Heath, C.I.E., M.C., transferred from the 14th Punjab Regiment. He was appointed permanent commandant in December 1929.

In 1929 the Battalion was reorganised into three rifle companies, one machinegun company and a headquarter wing, with a total fire power of sixty-one rifles, twelve Lewis guns and six machineguns (increased to eight guns in 1931). In 1930 the regimental brass band was abolished and a pipe band raised to take its place. In the same year the Battalion for the third time, was the winner of the Punjab Native Army Hockey Tournament.

NOWSHERA, 1929–1933

The 1/11th Sikhs were stationed at Nowshera for four years, which were by no means uneventful.

There was much political unrest in India in 1930, and in the Peshawar district seditious activity was stimulated under the leadership of one Abdul Ghaffar and his organisation of Red Shirts. At the end of April serious riots broke out in Peshawar city. On 5 May the 1/11th Sikhs, four hundred and fifty rifles strong, were moved by train from Nowshera to reinforce the garrison of Peshawar. There the Battalion was held as a reserve under the direct orders of the district commander. It was not called upon to participate in the restoration of order in Peshawar city, but was soon utilised to assist the civil authorities in the district.

On 11 May B Company was despatched with the 15th/19th Hussars to Charsadda, where, in spite of the arrest of Abdul Ghaffar, his Redshirt army was rapidly increasing and the cry of revolution was daily becoming more popular. B Company rejoined in Peshawar a week later; but a second call was received from the same area, and this time A Company went to join the Risalpur Cavalry Brigade at Charsadda.

The internal unrest spread to the Mohmand frontier, where the border villages had the passive support of a Mohmand *lashkar* in the cave area around Mir Ghazab within a few miles of the disaffected villages of Matta Mughal Khel and Shabkadar. On the afternoon of 30 May, in stifling heat, the 1/11th Sikhs (less A Company) and 16th Mountain Battery R.A. marched out from Peshawar for Shabkadar Fort. After bivouacking for the night on the bank of the Kabul River at Nagoman, they marched into Shabkadar next morning. Here A Company rejoined headquarters.

The Battalion encamped in a grove of trees outside the walls of the fort, which was already occupied by the 3/17th Dogra Regiment.

The next two weeks formed a period of continuous activity for the troops at Shabkadar. While the Royal Air Force were entrusted with the task of harassing the Mohmand *lashkar* just across the border, the troops were at first chiefly employed in assisting the civil authorities to secure the arrest of political firebrands in the district. The efforts of the Royal Air Force to dislodge the Mohmand *lashkar* proved unsuccessful, however, and after a short time the mountain battery started to shell one of the more prominent cave areas.

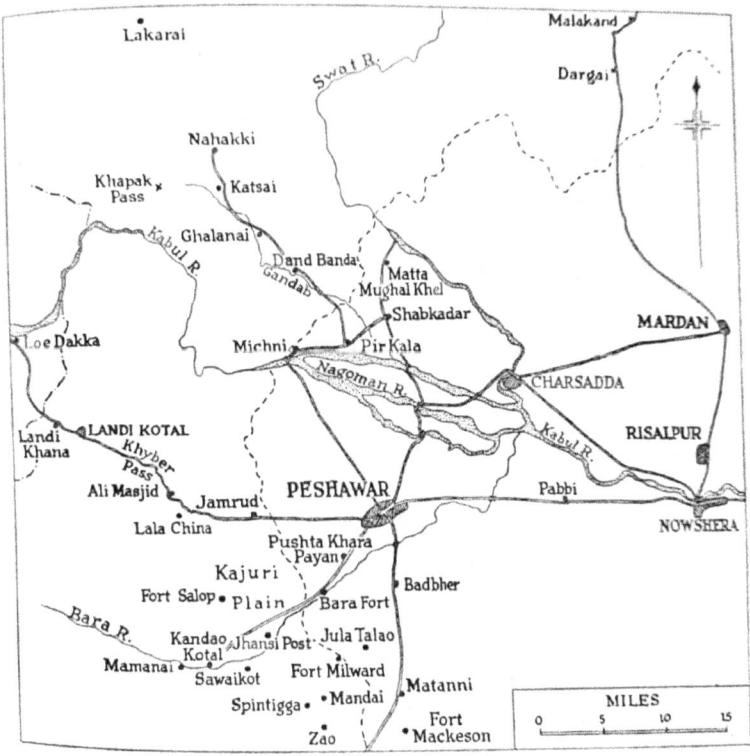

THE PESHAWAR AREA.

On 9 June the 1/11th Sikhs formed the escort to the battery which, in order to get within shrapnel range of some parties who had moved to the crest of a hill, advanced slightly beyond the frontier blockhouse line. This advance induced about two hundred of the Mohmands to move forward from the line of the frontier foothills, and the Sikhs became engaged with them at long range. During our subsequent retirement, the Mohmands advanced with great rapidity to the blockhouse line and offered good targets to our rearguard, which inflicted a number of casualties on the enemy without loss to itself.

This skirmish, trifling though it was, had the effect of dispersing the Mohmand *lashkar*. Meantime, the Peshawar district had been invaded by an Afridi *lashkar*, and then came news of a hostile gathering on the Utman Khel frontier north of the Swat River. The 1/11th Sikhs were sent off to join a column under Brigadier Fordham, which was formed to deal with the latter menace. Operations, though arduous, lasted for only five days; and the Battalion came in for no actual fighting. On 23 June the Sikhs were back in Peshawar, where they joined the Nowshera Column. The first invasion of Afridis had meanwhile petered out, and for six weeks the situation remained quiet.

Early in August it became known that the Afridis were collecting a *lashkar* for a second invasion. When the *lashkar* was thought to be within striking distance, the 1/11th Sikhs found themselves holding an extended outpost line from the Bara River to the Khyber railway astride the waterworks at Pushta Khara Payan. This outpost line was avoided by the Afridis, who started their infiltration into British territory on 6 August. The Afridi bands, of considerable strength, made full use of the sympathetic attitude of the villagers and the inhabitants of Peshawar city, and of the wonderful cover afforded by standing crops; they proved most difficult to locate and bring to bay. The Sikhs remained on outpost duty until 11 August, when they returned to Peshawar. During the next few days they participated in several abortive excursions with the Nowshera Column in an endeavour to come to grips with the enemy. However, by 15 August the Peshawar district was definitely clear of the Afridis. The heat had been intense, but the troops showed remarkable zest in carrying out their duties.

FRONTIER OPERATIONS, October 1930-March 1931

As a result of these Afridi incursions, the Government of India decided to deny to those tribesmen the free use of the Khajuri and Aka Khel plains by establishing a blockade line, and further, to construct across the two plains a network of motor tracks so as to facilitate the rapid movement of troops. The forces which moved out in October 1930 to effect this object included the Jhansi, Rawalpindi and Nowshera Brigades. The two former, in the first instance, were entrusted with the occupation of the Khajuri plain; whilst to the Nowshera Brigade, assisted by Frontier Constabulary, fell the task of establishing a blockade line from Jamrud to Fort Mackeson (on the Peshawar-Kohat road) on a frontage of twenty miles.

For some time the 1/11th Sikhs were employed almost exclusively in maintaining the blockade from Bara Fort to Matanni. During most of this period one company was stationed at Bara Fort for the protection of the advanced base camp, while the remainder of the Battalion was encamped at Jula Talao. Blockade work involved very heavy night duty. By day it was possible to watch the whole front with a few standing patrols pushed well forward towards the administrative border; but by night the number of patrols had to be more than doubled and they had to be increased in strength. The blockade proved effective. After hostile parties had been ambushed and surprised on several occasions, there is no doubt that the Afridis resorted to obtaining their supplies through the Kohat Pass Afridis who were outside the scope of the operations.

In November and December the Battalion supplemented its work on the blockade line by constructing many miles of motor track, and further variation was introduced by frequent reconnaissances into the hills in the direction of Zao. When acting independently on 8 December, the Battalion had an encounter with Afridis in the Mandai defile. On this occasion some tribesmen followed up our withdrawal, but paid for their temerity by losing several casualties.

The Battalion was in action again on 2 January 1931, but the enemy this time kept at a respectful distance.

On 5 January the 1/11th Sikhs were relieved of their duties in the blockade line by the 3/17th Dogras and went into camp at Garhi Jani with the remainder of the Nowshera Brigade (i.e. 2nd Essex Regiment, 2/13th Frontier Force Rifles and 8th Mountain Battery R.A.). During its stay of three weeks at Garhi Jani the Battalion was employed on road-making (which entailed the excavation of some deep cuttings and the shingling or rough metalling, of several miles of track), road-protection duties and bi-weekly operations up the Zao valley. There were five engagements with the Afridis. The most noteworthy operation was that carried out on the night of 12 January, when the 1/11th Sikhs moved independently of the remainder of the brigade across nearly five miles of very broken trans-border country and surrounded before dawn the village of Algadi. The ground had not been reconnoitred previously, but the Battalion had the aid of an excellent photographic mosaic prepared by the Royal Air Force. At Algadi, thanks to the bold initiative of two sepoys, the whole of a party of Afridis engaged in the Kohat Pass smuggling traffic were killed or captured. Algadi was then burnt to the ground and the Battalion, linking up with the remainder of the brigade which had been operating against Zao, withdrew without loss to camp.

From Garhi Jani the 1/11th Sikhs moved to New Bridge Camp (subsequently named Jhansi Post) on the left bank of the Bara River and there remained with the Nowshera Brigade till the conclusion of operations on 23 March. Road-making went on, various posts were constructed and a series of operations continued until no village in the fringe hills barring the way to Tirah remained unvisited. On two occasions night operations were successfully carried out, again with nothing except air photographs to assist directing companies to their objectives across the tangled foothills.

The final operation took place on 18 March, when the Nowshera Brigade carried out a reconnaissance over the Kandao Pass as far as the ridge which overlooks the Bara valley from Sawaikot to Mamanai at a range of about twelve hundred yards. Piqueting up to the summit of the pass was carried out successively by the 2/13th

Frontier Force Rifles and 1/3rd Gurkhas: the 1/11th Sikhs then found piquets up to the final objective, on which their advanced piquets were reinforced by two companies of the 3/17th Dogras. No opposition was encountered during the advance, but soon after reaching our objectives our piquets on the east flank were engaged. The withdrawal to the summit of the pass, over exceptionally intricate bush-covered ground, was closely pressed; and it was during the final stage of the retirement that a sepoy of the 1/11th Sikhs was wounded – the first and only casualty sustained by the Battalion in the course of the operations.

On 23 March 1931 the Nowshera Brigade, having handed over the completed line of permanent posts and piquets to battalions of the Khyber and Peshawar Brigades, marched in to Peshawar. Thence it went on to Nowshera, reaching its cantonment after an absence of forty-six weeks.

The 1/11th Sikhs had earned an enviable reputation for efficiency, and the fine spirit of the men was everywhere a matter of comment. The final remarks in the annual inspection report on the Battalion by the Commander of the Nowshera Brigade, Brigadier C. A. Milward, are worth quoting:

> In the field the Battalion moves exceptionally well and on some twenty-five operations it has always carried out to my complete satisfaction the role allotted to it. It works fast over very bad country, co-operates with other arms and units, conforms and carries out its part in brigade with a minimum of orders. It proved itself most reliable in face of the enemy and I felt complete confidence always. At work, making miles of roads and posts, it proved itself pre-eminent. The keenness, zest and skill of the men in this was beyond praise. The officers are a most excellent body. Their excellence is reflected in the men. I cannot speak too highly of the loyalty displayed and the devoted service to Government carried out by this battalion during the past and highly testing year. The spirit displayed by all ranks under most trustworthy Indian officers, against 'Redshirts', Congress, Utmen Khels and Afridis, in the hot weather and cold and work and all duties, has been simply magnificent.

In connection with the frontier operations from October to March 1931, the 1/11th Sikhs received the following decorations and awards:

> To be Brevet Colonel: Lieutenant Colonel L. M. Heath, C.I.E., M.C.
> Mentioned in Despatches: Lieutenant Colonel L. M. Heath, Captains C J. B. Church and A. E. Belchamber, Subadar Major Sapuran Singh, Subadar Maghar Singh and two sepoys. These two sepoys were awarded the Indian Distinguished Service Medal for conspicuous gallantry and initiative on the night of 12 January 1931.

The summer of 1931 was peaceful for the Nowshera garrison, and it was not till December that normal routine was interrupted by the decision of the Government of India to break up the Red Shirt organisation, which had been allowed to carry out its subversive activities without interference throughout the lengthy period of the 'Round Table' armistice. From Christmas Day onwards for about six weeks a minimum of two companies of the 1/11th Sikhs were continuously employed in aid of the civil authorities and police.

CHITRAL EMERGENCY COLUMN, September-October 1932

In September 1932 the Battalion was again engaged in frontier operations as part of the Chitral Relief Column,[23] which was commanded by Colonel Heath, who was temporarily in command of the Nowshera Brigade. The 1/11th Sikhs were commanded by Captain H. V. Spankie, M.C. The role of the column was to assist the Nawab of Dir to deal with insurgent tribesmen who had assembled to interfere with his protection of the Chitral road along which the ordinary Chitral relieving column was due to pass in mid-September, returning in early October.

---

[23] The Column included one squadron and machine gun troop of the 20th Lancers, one section 4th Mountain battery, R.A., one section 1st Armoured Car Company, the 1/11th Sikhs, Guides Infantry and the 2/9th Gurkha Rifles.

The Emergency Column left Nowshera on 6 September and, after an uneventful march, arrived at Bandagai on the 13th, where it established itself in a perimeter camp. Piqueting and protective measures were carried out along the Chitral road. The column remained at Bandagai for five days. The camp was heavily sniped every night; but, owing to the way in which tents had been dug down and the perimeter strengthened, very few casualties to personnel were sustained, though the animals did not escape so lightly; camp piquets were also attacked on several occasions.

Our troops laid a number of ambushes, several of which were successful and entailed severe losses to the tribesmen. In one of these, on the night of 15 September, Jemadar Arjan Singh distinguished himself. Though shot through the thigh, he continued to command his men, who remained unaware that he was wounded. For his gallantry he was later awarded the Indian Order of Merit, 2nd Class.

The Chitral reliefs passed through Bandagai on 16 September, and on the 18th the camp site of the Emergency Column was changed to a less exposed position. Thereafter, no incident of importance occurred. The relieved Chitral troops passed through on 10 October, and four days later the Emergency Column began its return march. Nowshera was reached on 18 October. The casualties suffered by the Emergency Column totalled thirteen in all, the 1/11th Sikhs having four men wounded.

For 'distinguished service in the field' during the above operations Colonel Heath was awarded the Distinguished Service Order; the same officer, Captain Spankie, Subadar Thakur Singh and a naik of the 1/11th Sikhs were mentioned in despatches.

THE COLOURS, 1933

On 20 March 1933 new Colours were presented to the 1/11th Sikhs by Mr. G. Cunningham, Acting Governor of the North-West Frontier Province, at a special ceremonial parade. Many pensioned Indian officers and other ranks came up from their homes to witness the ceremony.

The new Colours bear the battle-honours of the 11th Sikh Regiment, as a whole. On 6 April the old Colours, which, of course, were inscribed with the battle-honours of the old 14th Sikhs[24], were taken by a special Colour party to Dehra Dun; there they were handed over with fitting ceremony to the Indian Military Academy to be laid up in the Chetwode Hall of that institution.

Colonel L. M. Heath left the Battalion on 6 April on appointment as instructor at the Senior Officers' School, Belgaum; and Major C. L. Andrewes, M.C., took over command. He became permanent commandant on 6 December 1933.

MOHMAND OPERATIONS, August-September 1933

Prior to this, the 1/11th Sikhs took part in the operations against the Upper Mohmands in August and September 1933. These operations, under the control of Major General W. Dent, were carried out by two brigade columns composed entirely of Indian troops. Detachments of the Royal Air Force cooperated. Our troops advanced methodically up the Gandao valley towards the Nahakki Pass, covering the construction of a motor road into Mohmand territory.

The 1/11th Sikhs moved by train from Nowshera to Peshawar on 29 July. Next day troops of the Peshawar Brigade were transported to the Mohmand border. On the afternoon of the 31st the Sikhs were carried in lorries to Pir Kala, four miles west of Shabkadar on the road from that place to Michni. At Pir Kala work had already begun on the construction of a motor road northwards, and the leading troops of the Peshawar Brigade had moved forward to Dand Banda in the Gandao valley. The weather was, of course, extremely hot.

On 2 August the 1/11th marched forward to Dand Banda, there relieving the Guides Infantry, who advanced next day to join the

---

[24] Namely, Lucknow 1857–58 Defence and Capture, Ali Masjid, Afghanistan 1878–79, Defence of Chitral, China 1900.

Peshawar Brigade at Ghalanai. The 1/11th remained throughout August at Dand, which became the headquarters of the Nowshera Column. The camp at Dand lay in a restricted space in a hot and airless hollow of the hills. Though the camp was vulnerable to hostile snipers, the rest of the troops was disturbed on only two nights in the month and only one casualty was incurred.

While the construction of the motor road proceeded the existing mule track was used daily by a convoy of pack animals required to maintain the Peshawar Column at Ghalanai. This necessitated the protection of the road, and the 1/11th Sikhs were employed on this duty – daily up to 10 August and thereafter for three days at a stretch alternately with the 3/2nd Punjab Regiment. The task involved leaving camp at about 5:30 a.m., establishing piquets on each side of the road, remaining out in the sun all day and getting back to camp between 6 and 7 p.m. Only one incident occurred to break the monotony of this road-protection duty. On 13 August, just after the withdrawal had begun, a small party of tribesmen fired upon a piquet of the 1/11th and killed one sepoy.

By 1 September the new motor road was ready for traffic up to Ghalanai, and on that date the Sikhs moved thither, being followed four days later by the remainder of the Nowshera Brigade. The 1/11th Sikhs provided a guard-of-honour at a *jirga* held by the Governor of the North-West Frontier Province on 3 September. On the 9th and 10th the Battalion constructed a permanent piquet, christened Ridge Piquet, on the road to Katsai; when completed, the post was garrisoned by one platoon.

On 11 September the Battalion, with the 2nd (Derajat) Mountain Battery and other details, moved to a camp at Katsai some five miles forward of Ghalanai and the same distance short of the Nahakki Pass. The site of the camp, situated in a re-entrant of the hills, was much intersected by nullahs, ten to twelve feet deep. These nullahs, though incommoding movement within the camp afforded good cover during the nightly efforts of hostile snipers.

For about a week the Battalion was employed in protective duty covering the construction of the road forward from Katsai. On 12 September two sepoys were wounded, one mortally. On the evening of the 15th a British aeroplane made a forced landing about a mile away from the Katsai camp. Two platoons from each company turned out immediately and, under heavy fire from the tribesmen on the hills, brought in the pilot and gunner, who were both unhurt. Captain J. V. Gordon and two Indian ranks received immediate awards of the Military Cross and Indian Distinguished Service Medal, respectively, for their gallant action in dashing ahead of the troops and actually effecting the rescue.

On 16 September the Peshawar Brigade moved out from Ghalanai to cover the salvage of the aeroplane. Tribesmen followed up the withdrawal of the brigade in the afternoon and, later, engaged Ridge Piquet with fire. The piquet was held by one platoon under Jemadar Sundar Singh, who reported at 6:15 p.m. that a havildar had been shot dead. Heavy hostile fire was directed against the piquet during the night until about 2 a.m., but a close attack was held off – largely owing to the assistance rendered by Number 2 Mountain Battery, which kept a gun laid on and opened fire whenever the piquet commander called for support. Jemadar Sundar Singh was awarded the Indian Distinguished Service Medal for his skilful and stout hearted defence.

The Battalion left Katsai camp and returned to Ghalanai on 18 September. The Mohmands now accepted the British terms, and operations came to an end; but for the next week or so, the 1/11th Sikhs were frequently employed on protective duties whilst the motor road was being completed up to Yusuf Khel. The Peshawar Brigade marched back on 28 September and the Nowshera Brigade followed on 3 October, arriving in Nowshera two days later.

In connection with the Mohmand operations Major Andrewes, Captain C. J. B. Church, Jemadar Sundar Singh and two other ranks of the 1/11th Sikhs were mentioned in despatches.

MOVE TO THE KHYBER

On 21 October 1933 the Battalion marched out of Nowshera on transfer to the Khyber Brigade.

APPENDICES

APPENDIX I, Commandants, 1846–1933

(Note: The Ranks stated are those held by the Commandants at the conclusion of their tenure of regimental command.)

Captain G. Tebbs	1 Aug. 1846 –12 Jan. 1852
Major T. E. Colebrooke [25]	13 Jan. 1852–7 Feb. 1855
Lieutenant Colonel J. Brasyer, C.B.[26]	8 Feb. 1855–May 1860
Captain A. W. Montagu	May 1860–June] 1861
Colonel C. C. G. Ross[27]	4 June 1861–31 Aug. 1875
Colonel L. H. Williams[28]	1 Sept. 1875–30 May 1884
Colonel G. N. Channer, V.C.	31 May 1884–30 Sept. 1888
Colonel W. V. Ellis[29]	1 Oct. 1888–24 Aug. 1895
Colonel J. W. Hogge, C.I.E., p.s.c.[30]	25 Aug. 1895–24 Aug. 1902
Colonel W. E. Bunbury[31]	25 Aug. 1902–24 Aug. 1908
Lieutenant Colonel H. J. Jones, D.S.O.	25 Aug. 1908–24 Aug. 1913
Colonel P. C. Palin, C.B.[32]	25 Aug. 1913–7 Aug. 1916
Lieutenant Colonel E. S. Earle[33]	8 Aug. 1916–7 Aug. 1920
Lieutenant Colonel J. G. Cadell, D.S.O.[34]	29 Nov. 1921–28 April 1924
Lieutenant Colonel F. G. Swayne	1 Feb. 1925–28 Oct. 1927
Lieutenant Colonel H. F. Story	29 Oct. 1927 – 5 Dec. 1929
Colonel L. M. Heath, C.I.E., D.S.O., M.C.	6 Dec. 1929 – 5 Dec. 1933

---

[25] Captain when appointed Commandant.
[26] Lieutenant when appointed Commandant.
[27] Major when appointed Commandant.
[28] Major when appointed Commandant.
[29] Lieutenant Colonel when appointed Commandant.
[30] Lieutenant Colonel when appointed Commandant.
[31] Lieutenant Colonel when appointed Commandant.
[32] Lieutenant Colonel when appointed Commandant.
[33] After Lieutenant Colonel Earle vacated command, Colonel H. S. E. Franklin, C.M.G., D.S.O. was appointed Commandant, but he never actually joined the Battalion, and during the interim the following officers officiated in command: Major G. Channer, D.S.O.; Captain R. A. Savory, M.C.; Major J. A. S. Daniell, D.S.O., O.B.E.; Lieutenant Colonel Hughes, M.C.
[34] After Lieutenant Colonel Cadell vacated command Lieutenant Colonel B. H. Finnis was appointed Commandant, but never actually joined the battalion, Major F.G. Swayne officiating in command until appointed Commandant.

Lieutenant Colonel C. L. Andrewes, 6 Dec. 1933-
M.C., p.s.c

APPENDIX II,

British Officers
The 14th King George's Own Ferozepore Sikhs
29 October 1914

Officers actually with the Battalion:

Lieutenant Colonel P. C. Palin, Commandant
Lieutenant Colonel F. A. Jacques, Second in Command
Major G. D. P. Swinley
Captain A. W. McRae
Captain G. Channer
Lieutenant L. R. Fowle
Lieutenant L. F. Cremen, Adjutant
Lieutenant M. D. Spankie, Quartermaster
Lieutenant R. J. F. P. Meade
2nd Lieutenant R. A. Savory
Lieutenant H. J. M. Cursetjee, Medical Officer
Indian Medical Service

Officer Commanding the Depot at Multan:
Captain D. M. Field (Political Department)

Officers extra-regimentally employed:
Major E. S. Earle, Adjutant, Kolar Gold Fields Volunteers
Captain F. E. G. Talbot, p.s.c.G.S.0.2., Army Headquarters
Captain H. G. Wilmer, p.s.c., Staff Captain, 29th Indian Infantry Brigade

Officers on leave in England at Outbreak of War and retained for services in Europe:
Captain J. A. S. Daniell
Captain M. Wace
Captain K. R. McCloughin
Lieutenant C. McD. Allardice

APPENDIX III, War Casualties 1914 – 1919

BRITISH OFFICERS, Killed, or Died of Wounds:

Major G. D. P. Swinley	13.5:15
Lieutenant M. D. Spankie	14.5:15
Lieutenant Colonel F. A. Jacques	4.6:15
Captain A. W. McRae	4.6:15
Lieutenant L. R. Fowle	4.6:15
Lieutenant L. F. Cremen	4.6:15
Lieutenant R. J. F. P. Meade	4.6:15
Lieutenant M. C. G. Mathew	4.6:15
2nd Lieutenant G. W. Hornsby	4.6:15
2nd Lieutenant W. H. Lowry	4.6:15
Lieutenant H. E. Masters	4.6:15
2nd Lieutenant S. V. Hasluck	4.6:15
Major H. G. Wilmer	5.7:15
Captain A. F. MacLean	8.8:15
2nd Lieutenant G. H. Whitfield	8.8:15
2nd Lieutenant A. Irving	26.10.18

Drowned
2nd Lieutenant C. J. Unger	19.8:15

Killed while serving with other Units:
Captain K. R. McCloughin (France)	1915
Lieutenant C. McD. Allardice (France)	1915
Lieutenant P. N. Gurdon (East Africa)	1916

Wounded
Lieutenant Colonel P. C. Palin	1.3:15
Captain G. Channer	13.5:15 and 26.10.18
Captain J. D. Strong	29.5:15
2nd Lieutenant R. A. Savory	4.6:15 and 26.10:15
2nd Lieutenant R. G. Wreford	4.6:15
Captain R. S. Engledue	28.6:15
Lieutenant H. J. M. Cursetjee, I.M.S.	28.6:15
2nd Lieutenant A. J. M. Reeves	7.8:15
Captain J. A. S. Daniell	8.8:15
Captain M. Saunders	8.8:15

Major F. A. Loudon	9.8:15
Captain G. F. Bunbury	26.10:15
Lieutenant K. K. O'Connor	26.10:15
Lieutenant C. J. B. Church	26.10:15
2nd Lieutenant D. W. G. Humphreys	26.10:15

Wounded while serving with another unit
Captain M. Wace	7.8:15

INDIAN OFFICERS, Killed, or Died of Wounds

Jemadar Partap Singh	Egypt
Jemadar Rur Singh	France
Subadar Major Lall Singh	Gallipoli
Subadar Kirpal Singh	Gallipoli
Jemadar Bir Singh	Gallipoli
Subadar Dhiyan Singh	Gallipoli
Subadar Sundar Singh	Mesopotamia
Subadar Gurmukh Singh (B.M.P.)	Mesopotamia

TOTAL INDIAN, ALL RANKS

	Indian Officers.	Other Ranks	Followers
Killed, or Died of Wounds	8	308	4
Drowned	1	78	2
Died of Disease		30	2
Total Deaths	9	416	8
Wounded	17	941	
Total	**26**	**1,357**	**8**

APPENDIX IV, Drafts Sent to the 14th Sikhs between 1 November 1914 and 28 May 1919

Indian Officers	Other ranks	Followers	Source
14	892	54	Depot, 14th Sikhs
1	61		45th Sikhs
	30		36th Sikhs
	259	9	15th Sikhs
7	496	4	Burma Military Police
2	98	5	87th Punjabis
2	57	3	82nd Punjabis
		21	Followers' Central Depot
Total 26	1,893	96	

In addition, two complete companies of the 1st Patiala Infantry (Imperial Service Troops) were attached to the battalion in Gallipoli.

By September 1919 4,600 men had been in the ranks of the battalion since 1914.

APPENDIX V, Subadar Majors 1864–1934

	Date of Appointment
Sekundar Khan, Bahadur, O.B.I.	29 January 1864
Didar Singh	1 May 1871
Nand Singh, Bahadur, O.B.I ..	21 May 1881
Suhel Singh, Bahadur, O.B.I., I.O.M.	1 May 1887
Man Singh, Sardar Bahadur, O.B.I., I.O.M.	18 June 1890
Mitt Singh	16 Jan. 1903
Atar Singh, Bahadur, I.O.M. .	1 December 1903
Hony. Capt. Bhagwan Singh, Sardar Bahadur, 0.B.I.,I.O.M.	16 September 1904
Lall Singh[35]	4 July 1914
Hony. Lieutenant Sham Singh, Bahadur, O.B.I., I.D.S.M	5 June 1915
Hony. Lieutenant Jaimal Singh, M.C.,	5 February 1920
Hony. Capt. Narain Singh, Sardar Bahadur, M.C., O.B.I., I.D.S.M. .	2 October 1920
Bogh Singh, M.C.	1 May 1927
Hony. Lieutenant Sapuran Singh, Bahadur, O.B.I	20 August 1929
Jaswant Singh, Sardar Bahadur, O.B.I	20 August 1934

---

[35] Killed in action, 4 June 1915.

OTHER BOOKS FROM GOSLING PRESS

A Record of the 58th Rifles F.F.in the Great War. 1914-1919
By Colonel A. G. LIND, D.S.O.

Vaughan's Rifles was originally raised in 1849 as the 5th Regiment of Punjab Infantry. Lord Kitchener's Indian Army reforms of 1903 meant that the Regiment's designation was changed to 58th, Vaughan's, Rifles (Frontier Force).

The Regiment was a mixed class regiment meaning that in 1914 the Regiment's class composition was three companies each of Pathans and Sikhs, and one company each of Dogras and Punjabi Muslims.

During the First World War the regiment was sent with Force A to France to serve with 21st Infantry Brigade, part of 7th Meerut Division. At the end of 1915 the Regiment was sent to Egypt where it initially served with 31st Indian Brigade and then in 1916 it was transferred to 20th Indian Brigade. It then served with the Egyptian Expeditionary force for the remainder of the war. Although one company was attached to PAMFORCE in East Africa during 1918.

.

Regimental History of the 1st Battalion 8th Punjab Regiment
by N M Geoghegan and M H.A. Campbell

The 89th Punjabis had a most distinguished record of service during the First World War. They have the unique distinction of claiming to have served in more theatres of war than any other unit of the British Empire in that conflict. These included: Aden (Yemen), Egypt, Gallipoli, France, Mesopotamia, North West Frontier of India, Salonika (Greece), and the Russian Transcaucasia, where they served from 1918-20 as part of the British Expeditionary Force

Operations of the Mounted Troops of the Egyptian Expeditionary Force
By W J Foster, J G Browne and Rex Osborne

The E.E.F. came into being in March 1916 from the remnants of the British troops from Gallipoli and the troops already in Egypt although it lost ten of its fourteen infantry divisions to other theatres in quick order. The multinational force of Australians, New Zealanders, Indians and British Territorial troops became a strategic reserve for the British Army

This fascinating book was originally published as a series of ten articles in the Cavalry Journal between 1921 and 1923. The articles were an attempt to bring together learning form what was probably the last major cavalry campaign.

The Life of Sir Stanley Maude Lieutenant General K.C.B, C.M.G., D.S.O.
By Major General Sir C. E. Callwell. K.C.B.

The life and achievements of General Sir Stanley Maude deserve to be better known, since today he is usually only known for his late arrival at the beach during the evacuation at Gallipoli and for the capture of Baghdad in 1917.

His greatest triumph was perhaps the capture of Baghdad in March 1917 although due to his untimely death in November 1917 from Cholera at the age of 53, it is perhaps eclipsed by General Allenby's capture of Jerusalem in December.

This study considers Maude's early postings in the Sudan and Boer Wars as well as his service in the opening phases of the Great War and his later triumphs, shedding light on a cautious and consistent, rather than a spectacular, commander.

All Gosling Press book are available direct from www.goslingpress.co.uk or from Amazon

www.ingramcontent.com/pod-product-compliance
Lightning Source LLC
Chambersburg PA
CBHW072054110526
44590CB00018B/3160